Wellbeing in Politics and Policy

Series Editors
Ian Bache
University of Sheffield
Sheffield, UK

Karen Scott
Exeter University (Cornwall Campus)
Penryn, Cornwall, UK

Paul Allin
Imperial College London
London, UK

Wellbeing in Politics and Policy will bring new lenses through which to understand the significance of the dramatic rise of interest in wellbeing as a goal of public policy. While a number of academic disciplines have been influential in both shaping and seeking to explain developments, the Politics discipline has been relatively silent, leaving important theoretical and empirical insights largely absent from debates: insights that have increasing significance as political interest grows. This series will provide a distinctive addition to the field that puts politics and policy at the centre, while embracing interdisciplinary contributions. Contributions will be encouraged from various subfields of the discipline (e.g., political theory, comparative politics, governance and public policy, international relations) and from those located in other disciplines that speak to core political themes (e.g., accountability, gender, inequality, legitimacy and power). The series will seek to explore these themes through policy studies in a range of settings—international, national and local. Comparative studies—either of different policy areas and/or across different settings—will be particularly encouraged. The series will incorporate a wide range of perspectives from critical to problem-solving approaches, drawing on a variety of epistemologies and methodologies. The series welcomes Pivots, edited collections and monographs.

More information about this series at
http://www.palgrave.com/gp/series/15247

Ian Bache

Evidence, Policy and Wellbeing

palgrave
macmillan

Ian Bache
University of Sheffield
Sheffield, UK

Wellbeing in Politics and Policy
ISBN 978-3-030-21375-6   ISBN 978-3-030-21376-3   (eBook)
https://doi.org/10.1007/978-3-030-21376-3

© The Editor(s) (if applicable) and The Author(s), under exclusive license to Springer
Nature Switzerland AG 2020
This work is subject to copyright. All rights are solely and exclusively licensed by the
Publisher, whether the whole or part of the material is concerned, specifically the rights
of translation, reprinting, reuse of illustrations, recitation, broadcasting, reproduction
on microfilms or in any other physical way, and transmission or information storage and
retrieval, electronic adaptation, computer software, or by similar or dissimilar methodology
now known or hereafter developed.
The use of general descriptive names, registered names, trademarks, service marks, etc. in this
publication does not imply, even in the absence of a specific statement, that such names are
exempt from the relevant protective laws and regulations and therefore free for general use.
The publisher, the authors and the editors are safe to assume that the advice and
information in this book are believed to be true and accurate at the date of publication.
Neither the publisher nor the authors or the editors give a warranty, expressed or implied,
with respect to the material contained herein or for any errors or omissions that may have
been made. The publisher remains neutral with regard to jurisdictional claims in published
maps and institutional affiliations.

This Palgrave Pivot imprint is published by the registered company Springer Nature
Switzerland AG
The registered company address is: Gewerbestrasse 11, 6330 Cham, Switzerland

ACKNOWLEDGEMENTS

This book draws on material from a number of projects but, in particular, research conducted for the Community Evidence Wellbeing programme of the What Works Centre for Wellbeing (grant reference ES/N003756/1). I am grateful to my programme colleagues for many useful insights and to those who gave their time to be interviewed.

I would like to thank Jemima Warren and Oliver Foster at Palgrave Macmillan for their support for the book and the series of which it is a part, and also to Karen Scott, Louise Reardon and Paul Allin for their very helpful comments on the manuscript. I have learned a great deal from working closely with Karen, Louise and Paul in recent years.

My greatest debt is to Gillian Elizabeth Cantrill—for many reasons. This book is dedicated to her memory.

CONTENTS

LIST OF TABLES

CHAPTER 1

Introduction

Abstract This chapter introduces the idea of pursuing wellbeing government through government policy and identifies the three main aims of the book, which are:

1. To understand the role of evidence in shaping the prospects for wellbeing in UK public policy.
2. To inform the barriers literature on the use of evidence in policy.
3. To inform the multiple streams approach (MSA) to agenda-setting.

It identifies the focus as developments at UK government level, although it indicates that the findings and arguments presented have wider significance.

Keywords Evidence · Wellbeing · UK · Multiple streams approach · Agenda-setting

> Emphasising the role of power and authority at the expense of knowledge and expertise in public affairs seems cynical; emphasising the latter at the expense of the former seems naïve. (Solesbury 2001, 9)

© The Author(s) 2020
I. Bache, *Evidence, Policy and Wellbeing*,
Wellbeing in Politics and Policy,
https://doi.org/10.1007/978-3-030-21376-3_1

INTRODUCTION

The idea of pursuing wellbeing through government policy can be traced back centuries but is one that has received renewed attention in recent times in the context of economic crises and seemingly intractable social and environmental challenges. This interest has led to new wellbeing measurement frameworks both within international organisations, such as the EU, OECD and UN, and in a diverse range of national and subnational contexts. The proliferation of new measurement frameworks and alternative indicators of progress has 'opened up space for discussion about society's end goals and how to achieve them, creating opportunities for those who question the focus on economic growth' (Hayden and Wilson 2018, 147). For some, these developments 'have the potential to bring about a real paradigm shift concerning what we as a society consider to be progress and how, as a consequence, we will shape how we live together' (Kroll 2011, 1). Ultimately, this could lead to a shift away from the dominant focus on economic goals, which has the pursuit of Gross Domestic Product (GDP)[1] growth at its apex, or at least the development of more public policies that focus on a broader set of concerns. At the level of specific policies, wellbeing analysis can provide an alternative (or complement) to established techniques for policy appraisal and evaluation that draw on the market-based techniques of neoclassical economics (Chapter 3).

In analysing developments, Bache and Reardon (2016) argued that while wellbeing measurement was 'an idea whose time had come', this was not yet the case in policy terms. However, they concluded that, in the UK, 'reluctance to embrace wellbeing in policy has been largely succeeded by interest in "what works" for wellbeing' in policy (Bache and Reardon 2016, 44). In this context, the accumulation and dissemination of scientific (or 'research based') evidence[2] on how policy might enhance wellbeing is seen as a crucial next step in pushing wellbeing further up the political

---

[1] Gross Domestic Product refers to the market value of goods produced within a country's borders. It succeeded GNP as the benchmark for economic growth in the early 1990. GNP refers to the total market value of goods and services produced by the residents of a country, even if they are living abroad. GDP and GNP are alternative ways of measuring the same phenomenon and have subjected to same criticisms relating to the dominant focus on economic growth.

[2] Scientific evidence is distinct from other forms of knowledge—political professional and experiential—that also influence policy-making (see Chapter 2). From here on, the terms 'scientific evidence' and 'evidence' are used interchangeably.

agenda. This prompted the government to co-fund a What Works Centre for Wellbeing (WWCW)[3] in 2015 to help perform this task.

In this context, this book takes up the analysis from where Bache and Reardon concluded, to analyse the role of evidence in taking wellbeing from an issue that has government attention to one that leads to significant policy change. In doing so, it draws on contributions from political science, policy theory and literature specifically on the evidence and policy relationship. The book has three main aims, each of which is discussed further below:

1. To understand the role of evidence in shaping the prospects for wellbeing in UK public policy.
2. To inform the barriers literature on the use of evidence in policy.
3. To inform the multiple streams approach (MSA) to agenda-setting.

While the book focuses on developments at UK government level,[4] a number of the findings and arguments presented here have wider significance, both in relation to wellbeing developments elsewhere and to the theoretical literatures on agenda-setting and evidence use.

This book draws on insights from a number of projects undertaken by the author in recent years,[5] but most specifically on interviews with policymakers and stakeholders that were undertaken as part of the work of the

[3]The 17 founding partners were: Economic and Social Research Council (ESRC); Department for Business Innovation and Skills; Department for Communities and Local Government; Department for Health; Department for Work and Pensions; Arts and Humanities Research Council; Department for Culture Media and Sport; Arts Council England; Sport England; English Heritage; Heritage Lottery Fund; Public Health England; Food Standards Agency; Cabinet Office; The Big Lottery Fund; Local Government Association; and the Office for National Statistics.

[4]While the focus here is primarily on developments relating to UK central government, it should be noted that there have been significant developments in relation to wellbeing in the devolved jurisdictions of Scotland, Wales and Northern Ireland. These are discussed in Chapter 6.

[5]These include those as Principal Investigator for the knowledge transfer project on *The Politics and Policy of Wellbeing* (2011) which was supported by the Higher Education Innovation Fund of the Higher Education Funding Council of England; and Principal Investigator for the seminar series on *The Politics of Wellbeing* (2013–2015), which was funded by the ESRC, Grant Reference ES/L001357/1.

Community Wellbeing Evidence Programme team for the WWCW.[6] The research design for the new empirical material is set out in Chapter 2.

SCIENTIFIC EVIDENCE AND AGENDA-SETTING

Scientific evidence has a particular status among forms of knowledge in the policy process, as the 'dominant language of legitimation and persuasion in today's liberal societies' (Goodwin et al. 2001, 15). Its use in policy-making has a long history, but this has intensified in recent decades, spawning a range of related literatures and a variety of terms to capture the processes involved. In the 1990s, the idea of evidence-based policy emerged as 'both a political slogan and an academic movement' (Botterill and Hindmoor 2012, 367) that sought to appeal to the notion of 'what works' in policy in an empirical sense rather than in terms defined by politics and values. Over time, the idea of 'evidence-based' policy has given way to other descriptions that seek to capture the nature of this relationship, such as 'evidence informed', 'evidence-aware' and 'evidence-inspired' (Chapter 2). One feature of developments in the UK has been the creation of 'What Works Centres' in particular policy areas,[7] most recently the WWCW, which indicated both the government's continuing emphasis on the role of evidence and also its ongoing interest in wellbeing.

Scientific evidence is used in various ways and at different stages of the policy process (Chapter 2), but there are relatively few studies of its role in agenda-setting (Chapter 4). Yet agenda-setting is arguably the 'most critical' stage of the policy process (Howlett et al. 2009, 92): one that shapes all subsequent stages. Wellbeing is a particularly apposite case for studying the use of evidence at the agenda-setting stage for two reasons.

---

[6] *Bringing Wellbeing to Community*, ESRC Grant Ref. ES/N003756/1 (Co-Investigator). The programme team consists of five universities (Liverpool, Durham, Leeds Beckett, London [Goldsmiths] and Sheffield) and five other organisations: Centre for Local Economic Strategies, Happy City, Locality, New Economics Foundation and Social Life.

[7] The first of these was the National Institute for Health and Care Excellence, which was established in 1999 to provide guidance on how to reduce the variability in the cost and availability of NHS treatment, and subsequently to produce national guidance and advice to improve health care. The other What Works Centres are in the areas of: crime reduction; early intervention; educational achievement; health and social care; improved quality of life for older people; and local economic growth. The centres aim to 'help to ensure that policy makers, practitioners and commissioners can make informed decisions based on impact and cost effectiveness' (Cabinet Office 2015).

The first is its position on the agenda as an issue that has the attention of government but one that has not led to significant policy action: in terms of agenda-setting theory, this situation represents the distinction between the *governmental* agenda and the *decision* agenda (Kingdon 2011). The second reason is that wellbeing is an issue where the government has clearly signalled the importance of scientific evidence in taking the idea forward in policy.

Much of the literature on evidence use in policy-making remains theoretically under-developed, and scholars have called for greater use of policy theory in this field (below). The MSA is adopted for this purpose as one of the most influential approaches to the study of public policy and arguably the dominant theoretical approach to understanding agenda-setting. The MSA is useful for highlighting the distinction between two kinds of evidence-based activity relating to first the nature of the problem and second the effectiveness of the solution (Cairney 2016, 32). While some consideration is given to the former in this book, the main focus is on the latter.

The MSA identifies three distinct processes or 'streams' of activity relating to problems, policy and politics, which operate relatively independently of each other but when brought together present the greatest opportunity for an idea to lead to policy action. Streams are brought together by 'policy entrepreneurs' when 'windows of opportunity' are opened by events in either the politics or problem streams. The MSA's particular combination of structure (the three streams) and agency (policy entrepreneurs) has proved remarkably robust and insightful for over three decades.

John Kingdon's foundational contribution on the MSA, first published in 1984,[8] has been cited over 20,000 times[9] and, through its focus on ambiguity in the policy process, 'seems to have become more relevant and suitable than ever before for the analysis of policy making in advanced democracies' (Zohlnhöfer et al. 2015, 412). One review of the literature in 2016 found a 'thriving field of study' (Cairney and Jones 2016, 53), while another suggested 'the model thrives in its application in exploring and describing the policy process across all continents' (Rawat and Morris 2016, 627).

[8] *Agendas, Alternatives, and Public Policies* (1984, 1995, 2011). The most recent edition has been used for this book (see References).

[9] 22,177 Google Scholar citations as of 30 May 2019.

Yet despite its prominent status, it is widely seen to be in need of development (Cairney and Jones 2016; Jones et al. 2016; Zohlnhöfer et al. 2015; Reardon 2018; Zahariadis 2014). Jones et al. (2016, 28), for example, refer to the failure of most studies to move 'beyond obligatory identification' of the MSA's core concepts, while Weible and Schlager (2016, 6) suggest that 'The MSA is at the empirical and theoretical crossroads of its development'. This book seeks to respond to the challenge of developing the MSA through focusing on the role of scientific evidence in agenda-setting. The MSA tends not to distinguish between scientific evidence and other forms of knowledge. Moreover, while the MSA does identify the importance of evidence in the form of 'indicators' in the problem and politics streams—the former in particular—its role in the policy stream is rather overlooked.[10] However, the contention here is that scientific evidence also plays a role in the policy stream, in particular by helping to demonstrate that ideas meet the criteria for survival. As such, evidence offers a potentially important resource to policy entrepreneurs in taking ideas forward.

Despite a rich political science literature on the role of knowledge in policy-making (Chapter 2), the literature on the *barriers* to the use of scientific evidence remains theoretically under-developed. Gough and Boaz (2015, 489) argued that 'Research on research use is still in its infancy and remains weak in theory', while Cairney (2016, x) observed that analysis is often 'underpinned by minimal policy theory'. Theories of the policy process consider the broad policy system within which evidence is used as their starting point rather than evidence use itself and, in doing so, highlights limitations of the barriers literature. Applying the MSA in this case draws attention to agenda-setting dynamics that can inform the barriers literature. These dynamics include: the length of time it can take for policy change to take place and the importance of windows of opportunity; the MSA criteria for survival that an idea has to meet if it is to survive the 'policy primeval soup'; and the role of policy entrepreneurs in mobilising evidence as a resource in framing problems and promoting their preferred solutions (Chapter 5).

---

[10]Some authors refer to 'information' in a broad sense, while a small number discuss evidence specifically. This is discussed in Chapter 5.

THE STRUCTURE OF THE BOOK

The book has five further chapters. Chapter 2 considers the use of scientific evidence in policy. In doing so, it distinguishes between scientific evidence and other forms of knowledge—professional, political and experiential (Head 2010). It also unpacks the notion of policy, suggesting that the role of evidence can vary across different policy levels, types and fields. The chapter identifies various reasons for the use of evidence in policy and explains the intensification of this use in recent decades and different terms and concepts developed to capture this relationship. It then provides an overview of extant research on other What Works Centre policy areas that informed the research design for the empirical material collected for this book.

Chapter 3 looks at the idea of wellbeing. It outlines some long-standing philosophical debates that inform contemporary developments. The chapter discusses the controversial notion of subjective wellbeing, which is seen to have a prominent place in UK policy thinking on wellbeing. It provides an overview of key developments in the rise of wellbeing in politics and policy both internationally and within the UK, leading up to the creation of the What Works Centre for Wellbeing in 2015. It then turns to the role of wellbeing in policy, providing examples of evidence on different drivers of wellbeing and on life satisfaction (a key indicator of subjective wellbeing). The chapter concludes by drawing together some of the key themes and issues that inform subsequent chapters.

Chapter 4 focuses on 'what works' for wellbeing, presenting the findings of original research on the use of scientific evidence on wellbeing in policy. It considers the importance of evidence relative to other forms of knowledge—political, professional and experiential. It identifies the accumulation of evidence as an important next step for wellbeing in policy, with considerable demand for scientific evidence of different types and for a range of purposes. The findings suggest the need for a broad understanding of 'what works' beyond the rational-technical sense often employed to describe the work of What Works Centres and in the use of evidence more generally.

Chapter 5 analyses the role of evidence in the policy stream as described in the MSA, again drawing on fresh empirical material. It outlines the main features of the MSA before considering the role of scientific evidence in the problem stream and, specifically, the role of indicators in bringing attention to the idea of wellbeing. It then discusses in more detail the role of evidence in the policy stream, structuring the discussion around the criteria for survival of a policy idea set out in the MSA. These criteria relate to technical feasibility, value acceptability, tolerable costs, public acquiescence and receptivity among elected decision-makers. The findings indicate that while evidence may have obvious relevance to some criteria for survival than for others, it plays a role across all of the criteria—some of which are more closely related than previously acknowledged.

Chapter 6 draws the book to its conclusion. It recaps the main findings and reflects on each of the three main aims of the book. In doing so, it considers the political appeal of wellbeing, the importance of how evidence is communicated and the ongoing challenges brought by the complex and contested nature of wellbeing. It also considers the significance of recent wellbeing initiatives internationally and nationally, including those in the devolved jurisdictions of Scotland, Wales and Northern Ireland.

Conclusion

The emergence of wellbeing onto government agendas around the world has led to the search for a greater understanding of what works for wellbeing in policy. In relation to this, scientific evidence is seen to have a particularly important role. Yet, as the epigraph opening this chapter suggests, it has been long acknowledged that evidence is only one of many factors that shape policy. In this context, this book draws on different analytical contributions to understand the role of evidence in taking the idea of wellbeing from one that has government interest to one leading to significant policy change.

The book takes up the challenge of using policy theory to inform the literature on the barriers to evidence use in policy. The use of the MSA and, in particular, the application of the subcomponents of the MSA policy stream, provides a unique contribution not only to the field of wellbeing but also to the study of evidence in policy. Through its application of the MSA, it draws attention to wider agenda-setting dynamics that contextualise the supply and demand problems that are often identified as the main barriers. In doing so, it offers a broader and more coherent perspective on the potential effectiveness of particular solutions proposed in response to these problems.

At the same time, this focus on scientific evidence in policy provides an excellent opportunity to reflect back on the theoretical components of the MSA, which tends not to distinguish evidence from other forms of knowledge and rather overlooks its role in the policy stream in particular. On these issues, the book highlights scientific evidence as a potentially important resource for policy entrepreneurs in both framing problems and in promoting their preferred solutions. As such, evidence can play a role in allowing policy entrepreneurs to couple the three streams of the MSA, which is central to an idea moving forward in policy.

References

Bache, I., & Reardon, L. (2016). *The Politics and Policy of Wellbeing: Understanding the Rise and Significance of a New Agenda*. Cheltenham: Edward Elgar.

Botterill, L., & Hindmoor, A. (2012). Turtles all the Way Down: Bounded Rationality in an Evidence-Based Age. *Policy Studies, 33*(5), 367–379.

Cabinet Office. (2015). *Government Guidance—What Works Network*. https://www.gov.uk/guidance/what-works-network. Accessed 8 September 2015.

Cairney, P. (2016). *The Politics of Evidence-Based Policy Making*. Basingstoke: Palgrave Macmillan.

Cairney, P., & Jones, M. (2016). Kingdon's Multiple Streams Approach: What Is the Empirical Impact of This Universal Theory? *The Policy Studies Journal, 44*(1), 37–58.

Goodwin, J., Jasper, J. M., & Polletta, F. (2001). Why Emotions Matter. In J. Goodwin, J. M. Jasper, & F. Polletta (Eds.), *Passionate Politics: Emotions and Social Movements* (pp. 1–24). Chicago: University of Chicago Press.

Gough, D., & Boaz, A. (2015). Editorial: Models of Research Impact. *Evidence and Policy, 11*(4), 450–489.

Hayden, A., & Wilson, J. (2018). Challenging the Dominant Economic Narrative Through Alternative Wellbeing Indicators: The Canadian Experience. In I. Bache & K. Scott (Eds.), *The Politics of Wellbeing: Theory, Policy and Practice* (pp. 143–168). Cham: Palgrave Macmillan.

Head, B. (2010). Reconsidering Evidence-Based Policy: Key Issues and Challenges. *Policy and Society, 29*, 77–94.

Howlett, M., Ramesh, M., & Perl, A. (2009). *Studying Public Policy: Policy Cycles and Policy Subsystems* (3rd ed.). Oxford: Oxford University Press.

Jones, M. D., Peterson, H. L., Pierce, J. J., Herweg, N., Bernal, A., Raney, H. L., et al. (2016). A River Runs Through It: A Multiple Streams Meta-Review. *The Policy Studies Journal, 44*(1), 13–36.

Kingdon, J. (2011). *Agendas, Alternatives, and Public Policies* (4th ed.). London: HarperCollins.

Kroll, C. (2011). *Measuring Progress and Well-Being: Achievements and Challenges of a New Global Movement*. Berlin: International Policy Analysis.

Rawat, P., & Morris, J. C. (2016). Kingdon's "Streams" Model at Thirty: Still Relevant in the 21st Century? *Politics & Policy, 44*(4), 608–638.

Reardon, L. (2018). Networks and Problem Recognition: Advancing the Multiple Streams Approach. *Policy Sciences, 51*(4), 457–476.

Solesbury, W. (2001). *Evidence-Based Policy: Whence It Came and Where Is It Going* (ESRC UK Centre for Evidence Based Policy and Practice, Working Paper No. 1), Queen Mary, University of London.

Weible, C., & Schlager, E. (2016). The Multiple Streams Approach at the Theoretical and Empirical Crossroads: An Introduction to a Special Issue. *Policy Studies Journal, 44*(1), 5–12.

Zahariadis, N. (2014). Ambiguity and Multiple Streams. In P. Sabatier & C. Weible (Eds.), *Theories of the Policy Process* (3rd ed., pp. 25–58). New York, NY: Westfield Press.

Zohlnhöfer, R., Herweg, N., & Rüb, F. (2015). Theoretically Refining the Multiple Streams Framework: An Introduction. *European Journal of Political Research, 54*(3), 412–418.

CHAPTER 2

Evidence and Policy

Abstract This chapter considers the use of scientific evidence in policy. In doing so, it distinguishes between scientific evidence and other forms of knowledge—professional, political and experiential. It also unpacks the notion of policy, suggesting that the role of evidence can vary across different policy levels, types and fields. The chapter identifies various reasons for the use of evidence in policy and explains the intensification of this use in recent decades and different terms and concepts developed to capture this relationship. It then provides an overview of extant research on other What Works Centre policy areas that informed the research design for the empirical material collected for this book.

Keywords Evidence · Policy · What Works Centre

> There is nothing a government hates more than to be well informed; for it makes the process of arriving at decisions much more complicated and difficult. (Keynes 1937, 409)

© The Author(s) 2020   11
I. Bache, *Evidence, Policy and Wellbeing*,
Wellbeing in Politics and Policy,
https://doi.org/10.1007/978-3-030-21376-3_2

INTRODUCTION

As noted in Chapter 1, scientific evidence has a particular status among forms of knowledge in the policy process, as the 'dominant language of legitimation and persuasion in today's liberal societies' (Goodwin et al. 2001, 15). It presents an appearance of neutral investigation that facilitates judgement between options not subject to partisan pressure. While such neutrality does not exist in reality, belief in the objectivity of evidence does often exist, and, as such, those advocating policy change can use the cognitive authority this offers to strengthen the validity of their frames (Knaggård 2015, 456). As Jaegher et al. (2000, 18) have argued, evidence 'serves as a powerful social resource to convince people that the expected factual implications of one groups' claims are in their best interest whereas the potential implications of the competing groups claims are not'. Evidence is used in policy-making in various ways—from helping to understand an issue, to identifying the appropriate policy response and shaping future thinking—and at various stages of the policy cycle, from creating, developing and implementing policy to defending and justifying a policy decision (Nutley et al. 2013, 10; GSRU 2007, 16–18). Yet, as the epigraph opening this chapter suggests, the use of evidence in policy and politics is far from straightforward.

The next section of this chapter explains the use of the term 'scientific evidence' and its various forms, before unpacking the notion of 'policy'. Section three turns to the use of evidence in policy and the idea of 'what works'. The fourth section reviews contributions to understanding the evidence-policy relationship, drawing on both broad political science conceptualisations and a more practitioner-oriented literature focusing specifically on the *barriers* to evidence use. It suggests that while both of these literatures contribute valuable insights, theories of the policy process can deepen insights on the use of evidence. Section five provides an overview of extant research on the use of evidence in six What Works Centre policy areas other than wellbeing, before the chapter concludes.

SCIENTIFIC EVIDENCE

In this book, scientific (or research-based) evidence is distinguished from other forms of knowledge—political, professional and experiential—that also play an important role in the policy process. *Political knowledge* refers to the strategies, tactics and agenda-setting abilities of political leaders and

Table 2.1 Two illustrations of simplified hierarchies of evidence based on study design (Nutley et al. 2013, 10)

• Level I: Well conducted, suitably powered randomised control trial (RCT) • Level II: Well conducted, but small and under-powered RCT • Level III: Non-randomised observational studies • Level IV: Non-randomised study with historical controls • Level V: Case series without controls. *Source* Bagshaw and Bellomo (2008, 27)	1. Systematic reviews and meta-analyses 2. RCTs with definitive results 3. RCTs with non-definitive results 4. Cohort studies 5. Case–control studies 6. Cross-sectional surveys 7. Case reports. *Source* Petticrew and Roberts (2003, 52)

their organisations, which set the 'big picture' of policy priorities and approaches; the *professional knowledge* of practitioners and managers is essential for understanding feasibility and effectiveness; and the *experiential knowledge* of service users and stakeholders is central to 'client focused' service delivery (Head 2010).

Scientific evidence can take a variety of forms, which are often presented in a hierarchy based on perceived strengths and weaknesses of different research designs. Typically, systematic reviews and randomised control trials (RCT) are placed at the top, with individual case studies at the bottom (see Table 2.1).

Evidence hierarchies are seen as a useful short cut for policy-makers seeking to judge the robustness of material offered to them. However, there are also problems with ordering evidence in such hierarchies, not least that they: can lead to a loss of potentially useful evidence by excluding all but the highest-ranking studies; pay insufficient attention to the need to understand what works, for whom, in what circumstances and why; and provide an insufficient basis for making recommendations about whether interventions should be adopted (Nutley et al. 2013, 11). We return to the role and significance of evidence hierarchies in the presentation of research findings on wellbeing in Chapters 4 and 5.

While there is a significant focus in both academic and practitioner-focused literatures on distinguishing between levels and types of evidence, the notion of policy does not usually receive similar attention. Yet it is important to pause to consider what we mean by 'policy' as the dependent variable in this relationship. Policy can mean many things in different contexts, which can have significant implications for the role of evidence.

POLICY: LEVELS, TYPES AND FIELDS

There is considerable divergence around how policy is defined. On a general level, policy might simply be understood as any course of action (or inaction) pursued by governments or other organisations. A more specific definition of public policy refers to:

> a set of interrelated decisions taken by a political actor or group of actors concerning the selection of goals and the means of achieving them within a specified situation where those decisions should, in principle be within the power of those actors to achieve. (Jenkins 1978, 15)

Thus, as Sanderson (2011, 69) notes, policy is not just specific instruments or legislation 'but covers a wide gamut of activities and processes from background ideas, through problem definition, development of strategies, identification of what has been effective elsewhere, implementation and review'.

Peter Hall's (1993) distinction between three orders of policy provided an influential heuristic for understanding the prospects for change at different *policy levels*: first-order change is relatively small scale, generally related to the settings of particular instruments; second-order change refers to changes to policy instruments but without shifting the overarching goals of policy; and third-order change refers to a shift in overarching goals. While first- and second-order changes might be considered normal policy adjustments within a stable paradigm, third-order change is generally associated with paradigm change and is thus least likely (Hall 1993, 278–279). Such distinctions are useful in relation to wellbeing. As noted in Chapter 1, wellbeing is an idea that might apply to policy at different levels. For some, it may be an opportunity to reorder the overarching goals of public policy away from a focus on dominant economic indicators, such as GDP (third-order change), while for others it could (or should) provide a route to changing various policy instruments (second-order change) or the settings of existing instruments (third-order change). At each level of policy, different sets of factors come into play and so the role of evidence is different, contending with a wider range of factors the higher the level of policy. In this sense, there is a hierarchy of policy as well as of evidence.

The literature on *policy types* suggests that more complex policy areas tend to be more receptive to evidence than less complex areas (Boswell 2012). Head identified the particular knowledge challenges faced by complex policy ideas:

> In relatively simple issues where all the variables can be specified and controlled, methodological rigour is likely to be tight, with some confidence that causal factors can be clarified. But in programs with multiple objectives, or where the clients/stakeholders are subjected to many sources of influence beyond the scope of the program, the challenge of accurate understanding is compounded. (Head 2010, 83)

In such cases, the way a problem is framed is important both for the scientific validity and for the political management of complex problems, which 'are unlikely to be "solvable" through a single policy instrument or "magic bullet"' (Head 2010, 83). It is for these reasons that wellbeing has been described as a 'wicked problem' (Chapter 3). Yet while the degree of complexity may be important in shaping perceptions of the need for evidence, as Boswell (2012, 23) suggests, 'it will reveal little about the function that research is playing in the policy process'. This is because the use of knowledge is often symbolic and, while policy-makers may draw on knowledge and expertise, this does mean that it will necessarily shape policy (below).

In relation to *policy fields*, it is useful to distinguish between three types that inform the state of knowledge and thus the role of evidence (Mulgan 2005). In *stable policy fields*, governments know most about 'what works' and there is a strong evidence base. Networks are well established, and the relevant professional bodies and experts can generally be relied upon to provide good advice. In *policy fields in flux*, the knowledge base is contested and there is disagreement over even the basic theoretical approaches. So while there is recognition that change is needed, there is no consensus on either the nature of the problem or the solution. In *inherently novel policy fields*, there is no strong evidence base because of the recent arrival of the issue to the policy arena. The differences between these types of fields highlight the importance of theory:

In the second and third categories, our questions are changing as well as our answers. In such situations, evidence does not exist in the abstract, floating free. It exists in relation to theories and concepts that provide the prisms through which the world is seen. These theories are not alternatives to hard facts and evidence: they are the only ways of making sense of them. (Mulgan 2005, 222)

In Mulgan's (2005) terms, wellbeing can be considered an *inherently novel* policy field in which less is known about 'what works' in policy than in more established fields. However, as wellbeing moves from an abstract idea to one that is being defined more precisely for use in policy, it also demonstrates characteristics of a policy *in flux*. These themes are picked up again in Chapters 3 and 4.

The Use of Evidence in Policy

While the use of evidence in policy-making has a long history, this has intensified in recent decades, spawning a range of related literatures and a variety of terms to capture the processes involved. A number of reasons have been identified for this intensification. One reason is that contemporary policy issues are increasingly complex in nature and/or stubbornly resist attempts to solve them (Bullock et al. 2001; Sanderson 2011). At the same time, the policy process has become more complex with the shift to governance (Rhodes 1997) and, increasingly, multi-level governance (Hooghe and Marks 2001; Bache et al. 2015), which requires coordination between an increasing number of actors across different venues and levels. In the context of greater complexity in both policy and governance, the increased demand for evidence became linked to the ongoing attempt by decision-makers to bolster their governing capacity and thus retain legitimacy as public scepticism towards politics increased. Greater openness of government information aimed at addressing this scepticism further increased the demand for evidence so that politicians would be more resilient in the face of criticism (Mulgan 2007, 580). As Bullock et al. (2001, 15) put it:

The world for which policy-makers have to develop policies is becoming increasingly complex, uncertain and unpredictable. The electorate is better informed, has rising expectations and is making increasing demands for services tailored to their individual needs. Key policy issues, such as social exclusion and reducing crime, overlap and have proved resistant to previous attempts to tackle them, yet the world is increasingly inter-connected and inter-dependent.

In some contexts at least, growing interest in 'what works' for policy has been a feature of a relatively non-ideological political climate (Mulgan 2005, 215). The case of the UK Labour governments between 1997 and 2010 illustrates this point. Labour stated in its 1997 General Election manifesto that 'what counts is what works' (Labour Party 1997, 2) and frequently adopted this mantra as part of its post-ideological Third Way doctrine. This approach was signalled clearly in a speech to the Economic and Social Research Council in 2000 by then Secretary of State for Education, David Blunkett. Blunkett stated that evidence was central to the development and evaluation of policy and that the government would 'not be guided by dogma but by an open-minded approach to understanding what works and why' (Blunkett 2000, 2). However, developments in the UK were by no means unique, with a range of other national governments and international bodies—including the European Union, United Nations agencies and the World Bank—moving in the same direction (Bannister and O'Sullivan 2013, 252). This movement was linked to a broader shift of managerial reforms focusing on effectiveness and efficiency, driven by a technocratic logic (Marston and Watts 2003, 147). The financial crisis intensified the drive for effectiveness and efficiency as 'value for money' became an even more important concept.

In short, the idea of evidence-based policy emerged as an appeal to the notion of 'what works' in policy in an empirical sense rather than in terms defined by values or ideology. While it was common in the 1990s to refer to 'evidence-based' policy, growing recognition of the many drivers of policy-making (e.g. GSRU 2007; House of Commons Science and Technology Committee 2006; see also below) shifted the discourse more towards *evidence-informed* policy to acknowledge that policy is rarely a simple and direct response to evidence. Other terms used to capture this shift include 'evidence-aware' policy (Davies and Nutley 2002), 'evidence-inspired policy' (Duncan 2005) and 'intelligent policy-making' (Sanderson 2011). Head (2010) developed a comprehensive account of why evidence should be seen as informing policy rather than constituting a 'systematic foundation' for the policy process. First, that a strong research base is simply not available to policy-makers in some areas; second, decision-makers are often motivated or influenced more by factors other than research evidence; third, that where evidence is available it is often poor; fourth, professional knowledge rather than evidence base is often more important; and fifth, evidence-based policy appears to have less influence in areas that are in flux (Head 2010, 80–81).

Most recently, the concept of 'knowledge mobilisation' has received increasing attention as a way of thinking through the complex processes relating to the uptake of evidence. It has meant 'moving away from top-down models of knowledge flows to an increasing recognition that the purposes for which knowledge is assembled, synthesised, borrowed and appropriated all matter' (Moss 2013, 237).

Understanding the Evidence-Policy Relationship

Significant political science contributions to the conceptualisation of the evidence-policy relationship can be traced back several decades and, in particular, to the seminal contribution of Carol Weiss (1979), which has shaped much of the subsequent debate (Dunlop 2014). In this litera-ture, it is commonplace to identify a continuum that places rationality at one end—where evidence is crucial in shaping policy—and politics at the other—where evidence is just one factor among a number, and generally not the most important (Marston and Watts 2003, 145; Cook 2011).

In setting the parameters for much of this debate, Weiss's (1979) article on typologies of knowledge utilisation identified seven meanings associ-ated with the use of research evidence in public policy. These ranged from the *knowledge-driven model*, which assumed a sequence of events through which research evidence leads directly to policy change, to a *political model* in which policy positions are shaped by interests or ideology and evidence is sought primarily as 'ammunition' to support a particular position. In a later paper, Weiss explained further the political dimension, suggesting that 'When new data or research findings arrive on the conference table in the councils of action they confront four I's already sitting at the table…ide-ology, interests, institutional norms and practices, and prior information' (Weiss 2001, 286)[1]. Weiss's *enlightenment model* received particular atten-tion for explaining how social research 'diffuses circuitously through man-ifold channels' (Weiss 1979, 429), whether academic, the media or policy networks. The model suggests that while it is rare for social research in par-ticular to lead directly to policy change, such research can have an important

---

[1] Here, ideology is taken to refer to people's 'basic values' and interests refer the self-interest of both people and organizations.

sensitising effect over the long-term that puts new issues on the agenda or changes the way an issue is viewed.

Christina Boswell developed Weiss's work on the political functions of knowledge to highlight evidence as 'a symbolic resource for underpinning the risky decisions of politicians, and bolstering the authority of embattled public authorities' (Boswell 2012, 251). Boswell (2008) distinguished between two symbolic functions: one being a legitimising function, in which an organisation uses knowledge to enhance its legitimacy in a particular policy area; the other a substantiating function, in which knowledge lends authority to help substantiate organisational preferences where there is political contestation. The legitimising function of knowledge is a theme emphasised by other scholars, with some arguing that the concept of evidence-based policy merely provides a smokescreen 'to obscure the reality of political manipulation in policy making' (Sanderson 2011, 62). This critical perspective has given rise to the use of the term 'policy-based evidence' to connote the legitimising function.

Generally, political scientists have long identified policy-making as an inherently political process and have taken this as starting point for seeking to understand more about how evidence is used in policy. As Head (2010, 83) argues:

> Policy decisions in the real world are not deduced from empirical-analytical models, but from politics and practical judgement. There is an interplay of facts, norms and preferred courses of action. In the real world of policy-making, what counts as 'evidence' is diverse and contestable. The policy-making process in democratic countries uses the rhetoric of rational problem-solving and managerial effectiveness, but the policy process itself is fuzzy, political and conflictual.

The difficulty of separating facts from values has been a particular feature of the debate. Majone (1989) emphasised the role of persuasion, suggesting that 'few arguments are purely rational or purely persuasive' and thus it is the blend between the two that matters. In this view, the role of policy analyst is one of marshalling arguments, more akin to that of a lawyer rather than an engineer or scientist. Argument is particularly important for securing policy change because of the inbuilt inertia within bureaucracies that give a comparative advantage to existing ideas and practices. Majone (1989, 48) suggests that:

An inappropriate choice of data, their placement at a wrong point in the argument, a style of presentation that is unsuitable for the audience to which the argument is directed – any one of these factors can destroy the effectiveness of information as evidence, regardless of its intrinsic cognitive content... the applicability of evidence depends on a number of features peculiar to a given situation, such as the nature of the case, the type of audience, the prevailing "rules of evidence," and even the persuasiveness of the analyst. (Majone 1989, 48)

This emphasis on the nature of a 'given situation' (or context) is a theme that resonates within both the academic and practitioner-focused literatures on evidence use.

The 'Barriers' Literature

Alongside this political science debate on the evidence and policy relationship has emerged a more practitioner-focused literature on the *barriers* to the use of evidence. This tends to focus on the distinction between supply and demand in the use of evidence and the relationship between the two. While acknowledging some of the issues raised in the political science contributions discussed above, this literature has been criticised for its tendency not to draw on theories of the policy process that might deepen insights on evidence use (Cairney 2016). For example, analysis of a systemic literature review by Embrett and Randall (2014) on the social determinants of health/health equity found that only seven of 6200 peer-reviewed articles published since 2002 drew on policy theory (Cairney 2016, 54). Based on Embrett and Randall's systematic review, Cairney (2016, 57–58) identified the top five barriers to evidence use as (in order): availability and access to research; clarity/relevance/reliability of research findings; timing and opportunity; policy-maker research skills; and costs. Some of these categories overlap considerably because they refer to the *relationship* between the supply of and demand for evidence.

Rutter's (2012) report for the Institute of Government on *Evidence and Evaluation in Policy-Making: A Problem of Supply or Demand*[2] is illustrative of this practitioner-focused literature. Rutter identified significant barriers on the supply side, including: academics finding it difficult to engage

---

[2] Her report summarised the findings of four seminars held at the Institute of Government and organised in collaboration with the Alliance for Useful Evidence and NIESR.

effectively with policy-makers; policies not being designed in a way that allows for evaluation; and a lack of useable data to provide the basis for research. Demand-side barriers included: problems with the timeliness and helpfulness of evidence and the mismatch between political timetables and those of evidence producers, allied to ethical reservations about experimentation; the fact that many decisions were driven by values rather than outcomes—and that 'evidence-drive' responses could bring significant political risk; and the lack of culture and skills for using rigorous evidence within the civil service (Rutter 2012, 16–17).

The UK Government Social Research Unit's report on *Analysis for Policy: Evidence-Based Policy in Practice* (GSRU 2007, 25) arrived at a similar list of factors shaping the use of evidence. It identified 'practical everyday issues' such as the timing, availability and presentation of evidence; resources available; and the trustworthiness of available evidence. These 'everyday issues' overlapped with 'more systemic' issues focusing on either the inadequate supply of or lack of demand for evidence. These included external pressures constraining the scope for analysis; the political timetable not matching research timetables; a reluctance to collect and analyse data for fear of unwelcome results; a lack of demand for fundamental and comparative analysis; a lack of overview of the bigger picture; and lack of long-term planning (GRSU 2007, 25–26). The important non-research factors were identified as political influence (e.g. manifesto commitments, ideology and changes in government/leadership); stakeholder influences (particularly those with close relationships with ministers and special advisers); and media and public influences, which were seen as particularly important on politicians, with a number of policy-makers suggesting that public perceptions were as important as hard evidence in securing support for policies (GSRU 13–14).

Such studies clearly have value in highlighting key issues in demand and supply and touch on wider issues. However, while there are some commonalities with the political science literature on the importance of political factors, the barriers literature does not draw on theories of the policy process that highlight other important dynamics. This not only impacts the quality of the analysis but also the effectiveness of the solutions proposed. As Cairney (2016, 110–111) notes, this has two main consequences: the first is that such studies tend to recommend the same solutions each time (e.g. workshops engaging both academics and policy-makers or making greater use of 'knowledge brokers'); the second is that despite many studies identifying similar barriers, the focus on supply and demand fails to provide a coherent explanation for the lack of policy progress.

The starting point for policy theory is not with a focus on the role of scientific evidence in policy but with a desire to understand how policy emerges, develops, changes or is discarded. Taking this wider view, 'the role of evidence, research and other types of knowledge can emerge as a constituent part of the analysis' (Ritter et al. 2018, 1540). As Cairney (2016) argues, policy theories draw attention to a policy process characterised by uncertainty, ambiguity and competition: one in which policy-makers have neither all of the available evidence, nor often the time to analyse what they have. This requires understanding of the heuristics they use in gathering evidence and also their biases towards particular forms of evidence, which may prove more important than the evidence itself. As Marmot (2004, 906–907) put it: 'scientific findings do not fall on blank minds that get made up as a result. Science engages with busy minds that have strong views about how things are and ought to be'. In this context, evidence use has to be understood both in relation to the way problems are 'framed' by policy advocates and also how they are understood by the policy-makers responsible for addressing them (Cairney 2016, 6).

Policy theory also draws attention to the complexity of the policy process, characterised by multiple actors and venues, in which policy competence is both shared and contested and evidence often has to address different audiences. In short, as Cairney (2016, 54) puts it: 'If we do not draw on theories that tell us how the policy process works, we will not know how the partial "removal" of one or more barriers will improve the links between evidence, policymaking, and policy'. As the focus of this study is on agenda-setting, the most relevant policy theory for this purpose is the multiple streams approach, which is the focus of Chapter 5.

RESEARCH ON 'WHAT WORKS': THE EVIDENCE ECOSYSTEM

Before concluding this chapter, it is useful to reflect briefly on research by John Shepherd (2014) aimed specifically at What Works Centre networks, given the interest of this book with the What Works Centre for Wellbeing. Moreover, the approach taken in Shepherd's research sought to go beyond the supply and demand distinction characteristic of most practitioner-focused studies to focus on the 'whole system' within a particular policy sector. The research, conducted before the creation of the WWCW in 2015, covers the use of evidence in six What Works Centre policy areas: crime reduction, health and social care; education; early inter-vention; ageing better; and local economic growth.

Shepherd's (2014) starting point is that the creation and adoption of effective policies depends on a 'functional evidence ecosystem' of which What Works Centres are an 'essential part'. As such, the Centres 'need to be concerned not just with evidence synthesis and adoption but with the whole system in their sector so that faults can be identified and put right' (Shepherd 2014, 5). Shepherd compares the evidence ecosystem to the supply chain from the petrochemical industry, with analogies to pumps, pipelines, usability, product blending, fuel, waste, viscosity and costs and his approach focuses on four features of this ecosystem: *evidence sources; trans-mission lines; problems;* and *incentives.* These domains are chosen because 'they cross ecosystem boundaries and facilitate the collection of information about evidence demand (evidence pull) and promotion (evidence push)' (Shepherd 2014, 22). Shepherd (2014, 11) identifies the three key ele-ments of the evidence ecosystem as: *a useful, relevant and dynamic evidence base* presented in a way that is usable for policy-makers, commissioners and practitioners; *supportive structures* that are dedicated to the effective transmission and uptake of evidence-informed interventions and policies; *a workforce able and motivated to apply evidence* for the improvement and commissioning of services. He argued that understanding the context and the audience is crucial to bringing about change through evidence use, for which there are three prerequisites: ability (knowledge and technical abil-ity, technology and resources); motivation (positive rewards and negative sanctions); and trigger (prompts at the point of decision) (Shepherd 2014, 18).

Shepherd's notion of the evidence ecosystem provides a useful bridge between theories of how the policy process works with the more specific focus of the barriers literature on supply and demand in the use of evi-dence. As such, the idea of the evidence ecosystem informs part of the research design for the empirical material collected for this book, alongside themes from the political science contributions on the use of knowledge. Following Shepherd's approach, interviewees were asked specifically about evidence sources; transmission lines; problems and incentives in the use of evidence (Chapter 4). This approach also provides the opportunity to com-pare the findings on wellbeing with Shepherd's findings across six policy areas (Chapter 4).

RESEARCH DESIGN

As noted in Chapter 1, this book draws on a number of projects undertaken by the author in recent years but most specifically on interviews with policy-makers and stakeholders that were undertaken as part of the work of the Community Wellbeing Evidence Programme team's work for the WWCW (see Chapter 1). Fifteen initial interviews were conducted with individuals from the national civil service (3); local government (3); charities (3); the voluntary sector (3); government agencies (2); and a non-departmental public body (NDPB) (1). The interviews were conducted by telephone and were recorded and transcribed. Three follow-up interviews and three additional interviews took place later in order to gain clarification on a number of points and to check for updates on developments.[3]

The target population consisted of individuals who had a close involvement with wellbeing in their work and the sample chosen to reflect a cross section of this estimated population of interest. Wellbeing is relatively new to many policy areas, and no systematic study has been undertaken to assess how many individuals across organisations are closely involved with wellbeing in their daily work. The selection of organisations was undertaken jointly with stakeholders from the WWCW who were close to the policy community and who were thus able to advise on relevant participants for this study. These connections facilitated access to senior actors who might otherwise have not been available for interview. While it was not the main aim of the research to identify differences in approach or emphasis across organisations, some differences did emerge and are reported in the following chapters.[4]

Interviews were the preferred choice of data collection in order to provide a deep understanding of the phenomenon of evidence use in complex policy arenas and to provide insight into the meanings of the subject's

---

[3]The initial interviews took place in August–September 2015 and were between 45 and 60 minutes long. The meaning of questions was clear to interviewees and no interviewees refused to answer any of the questions. The questions had been piloted with two policy actors who were part of the WWCW team. The follow-up interviews were conducted by telephone in 2016 and 2017 and the three additional interviews by telephone in August 2018. The research was approved by the Research Ethics Committee of the University of Sheffield and all participants completed a consent form, which allowed data to be used (anonymously) in publications.

[4]Although the small sample size for organisations of different types limits the generalisability of these comparative findings.

experiences. The use of semi-structured interviews ensured that the main themes and questions were addressed in all interviews but also treated the interviewees as 'active subjects' able to organise their responses within their own frameworks (Halperin and Heath 2012, 299).

In the first stage of analysing the findings, the interview transcripts were read holistically, looking at patterns in the data to facilitate the identification of important themes. The most important and interesting parts of the text were highlighted to provide a coding frame: all material was coded for relevant themes. The sections of text marked with each code were drawn together and conclusions drawn by analysing the meanings of the data and their implications for the research questions. The data from different respondents were cross-checked to validate key findings. Following analysis of the data, the initial findings were presented for verification to a workshop of WWWC stakeholders from a range of organisations and other policy-makers,[5] some of whom were interviewed for the research.

CONCLUSION

This chapter has explained the use of the term 'scientific evidence' in this book and has unpacked the notion of policy. It is important to do this because understanding the interplay of particular forms of evidence and the nature of the policy it is seeking to influence is a crucial part of understanding the role of evidence in policy. However, many other factors come into play, and with this in mind, the chapter has discussed contributions from political science and practitioner-focused literatures that highlight key themes that inform the analysis in subsequent chapters. The chapter also made the case for the use of policy theory in analysing the use of evidence, which draws attention to a spects of the policy process that are not covered in either the political science or barriers literatures, highlighting additional themes that are dealt with more fully in the discussion of the MSA in Chapter 5.

[5]This workshop took place on 5–6 October 2015, at Halifax Hall Hotel, University of Sheffield, Sheffield, UK.

REFERENCES

Bache, I., Bartle, I., Flinders, M., & Marsden, G. (2016). *Multi-level Governance and Climate Change: Insights from Transport Policy.* Lanham, MD and London: Rowman & Littlefield.

Bagshaw, S., & Bellomo, R. (2008). The Need to Reform Our Assessment of Evidence from Clinical Trials: A Commentary. *Philosophy, Ethics, and Humanities in Medicine, 3,* 23. https://doi.org/10.1186/1747-5341-3-23.

Bannister, J., & O'Sullivan, A. (2013). Knowledge Mobilisation and the Civic Academy: The Nature of Evidence, the Roles of Narrative and the Potential of Contribution Analysis. *Contemporary Social Science, 8*(3), 249–262.

Blunkett, D. (2000, February 2). *Influence or Irrelevance: Can Social Science Improve Government.* Speech to the Economic and Social Research Council.

Boswell, C. (2008). The Political Functions of Expert Knowledge: Knowledge and Legitimation in European Union Immigration Policy. *Journal of European Public Policy, 15*(4), 471–488.

Boswell, C. (2012). *The Political Uses of Expert Knowledge: Immigration Policy and Social Research.* Cambridge: Cambridge University Press.

Bullock, H., Mountford, J., & Stanley, R. (2001). *Better Policy Making.* London: Centre for Management and Policy Studies.

Cairney, P. (2016). *The Politics of Evidence-Based Policy Making.* Basingstoke: Palgrave Macmillan.

Cook, F. (2011, August 30–September 2). *Evidence-Based Policy-Making in a Democracy: Exploring the Role of Policy Research in Conjunction with Politics and Public Opinion.* Paper Presented for Delivery at the 2001 Annual Meeting of the American Political Science Association, San Francisco.

Davies, H., & Nutley, S. (2002). *Evidence-Based Policy and Practice: Moving from Rhetoric to Reality* (Discussion Paper No. 2). University of St. Andrews Research Unit for Research Utilisation.

Duncan, S. (2005). Towards Evidence-Inspired Policymaking. *Social Sciences, 61,* 10–11.

Dunlop, C. (2014). The Possible Experts: How Epistemic Communities Negotiate Barriers to Knowledge Use in Ecosystems Services Policy. *Environment and Planning C: Government and Policy, 32,* 208–228.

Embrett, M., & Randall, G. (2014). Social Determinants of Health and Health Equity Policy Research: Exploring the Use, Misuse, and Nonuse of Policy Analysis Theory. *Social Science and Medicine, 108,* 147–155.

Goodwin, J., Jasper, J. M., & Polletta, F. (2001). Why Emotions Matter. In J. Goodwin, J. M. Jasper, & F. Polletta (Eds.), *Passionate Politics: Emotions and Social Movements* (pp. 1–24). Chicago: University of Chicago Press.

GSRU. (2007). *Analysis for Policy: Evidence-Based Policy in Practice.* London: Government, Social Research Unit, HM Treasury.

Hall, P. (1993). Policy Paradigms, Social Learning, and the State: The Case of Economic Policymaking in Britain. *Comparative Politics, 25*(3), 275–296.

Halperin, S., & Heath, O. (2012). *Political Research: Methods and Skills*. Oxford: Oxford University Press.

Head, B. (2010). Reconsidering Evidence-Based Policy: Key Issues and Challenges. *Policy and Society, 29,* 77–94.

Hooghe, L., & Marks, G. (2001). *Multi-level Governance and European Integration*. London: Rowman & Littlefield.

House of Commons Science and Technology Committee. (2006). *Scientific Advice, Risk and Evidence Based Policy Making, Seventh Report of Session 2005–06* (Vol. 1). London: The Stationery Office.

Jaegher, C. J., Renn, O., Rosa, E. A., & Webler, T. (2000). *Risk, Uncertainty and Rational Action*. London and Sterling: Earthscan.

Jenkins, W. (1978). *Policy Analysis: A Political and Organizational Perspective*. London: Martin Robertson.

Keynes, J. M. (1937). *The Collected Writings of John Maynard Keynes* (Vol. 21). London: Macmillan.

Knaggård, Å. (2015). The Multiple Streams Framework and the Problem Broker. *European Journal of Political Research, 54,* 450–465.

Labour Party. (1997). *New Labour Because Britain Deserves Better, Labour Party Election Manifesto*. http://www.labour-party.org.uk/manifestos/1997/1997-labour-manifesto.shtml. Accessed 12 December 2018.

Majone, G. (1989). *Evidence, Argument and Persuasion in the Policy Process*. New Haven: Yale University Press.

Marmot, M. (2004). Evidence Based Policy or Policy Based Evidence? *British Medical Journal, 328,* 906–907.

Marston, G., & Watts, R. (2003). Tampering with Evidence: A Critical Appraisal of Evidence-Based Policy-Making. *The Drawing Board: An Australian Review of Public Affairs, 3*(3), 143–163.

Moss, G. (2013). Research, Policy and Knowledge Flows in Education: What Counts in Knowledge Mobilisation? *Contemporary Social Sciences, 3,* 237–248.

Mulgan, G. (2005). Government, Knowledge and the Business of Policy Making: The Potential and Limits of Evidence-Based Policy. *Evidence and Policy, 1*(2), 215–226.

Mulgan, R. (2007). Truth in Government and the Politicization of Public Service Advice. *Public Administration, 85*(3), 569–586.

Nutley, S., Powell, A., & Davies, H. (2013). *What Counts as Good Evidence?* Provocation Paper for the Alliance for Useful Evidence, Research Unit for Research Utilisation (RURRU), School of Management, University of St. Andrews.

Petticrew, M., & Roberts, H. (2003). Evidence, Hierarchies, and Typologies: Horses for Courses. *Journal of Epidemiology and Community Health, 57,* 527–529.

Rhodes, R. (1997). *Understanding Governance: Policy Networks, Governance and Accountability*. Buckingham: Open University Press.

Ritter, A., Hughes, C., Lancaster, K., & Hoppe, R. (2018). Using the Advocacy Coalition Framework and Multiple Streams Policy Theories to Examine the Role of Evidence, Research and Other Types of Knowledge in Drug Policy. *Addiction*. https://doi.org/10.1111/add.14197.

Rutter, J. (2012). *Evidence and Evaluation in Policy Making: A Problem of Supply or Demand?* Institute for Government Report. http://www. instituteforgovernment.org.uk/sites/default/files/publications/evidence%20and%20evaluation%20in%20template_final_0.pdf. Accessed 19 February 2015.

Sanderson, I. (2011). Evidence-Based Policy or Policy-Based Evidence? Reflections on Scottish Experience. *Evidence and Policy, 7*(1), 59–76.

Shepherd, J. (2014). *How to Achieve More Effective Services: The Evidence Ecosystem—Crime Reduction/Health and Social Care/Education/Early Interventions/Ageing Better/Local economic Growth*. Cardiff University/ESRC What Works Network.

Weiss, C. (1979, September–October). The Many Meanings of Research Utilization. *Public Administration Review, 39*, 426–431.

Weiss, C. (2001, July). *What Kind of Evidence in Evidence-Based Policy?* Third International Interdisciplinary Evidence-Based Policies and Indicator Systems Conference, CEM Centre, University of Durham.

CHAPTER 3

Wellbeing

Abstract This chapter looks at the idea of wellbeing. It outlines some long-standing philosophical debates that inform contemporary developments. The chapter discusses the controversial notion of subjective wellbeing (SWB), which is seen to have a prominent place in UK policy thinking on wellbeing. It provides an overview of key developments in the rise of wellbeing in politics and policy both internationally and within the UK, leading up to the creation of the What Works Centre for Wellbeing in 2015. It then turns to the role of wellbeing in policy, providing examples of evidence on different drivers of wellbeing and on life satisfaction (a key indicator of SWB). The chapter concludes by drawing together some of the key themes and issues that inform subsequent chapters.

Keywords Wellbeing · Subjective wellbeing · What Works Centre for Wellbeing · Life satisfaction

...because well-being can be measured, it allows us to use the language of evidence and efficiency as opposed to justice and idealism, and sometimes it is useful to couch arguments in these terms. It becomes possible to quantify a critique of capitalism, to quantify the size of its failure to deliver good lives as understood by many people. Progressives can translate a subversive critique, all too often ineffective because vague and apparently elitist, into

© The Author(s) 2020
I. Bache, *Evidence, Policy and Wellbeing*,
Wellbeing in Politics and Policy,
https://doi.org/10.1007/978-3-030-21376-3_3

the language of bureaucracy, evidence-based policy, quantified analysis. (Seaford 2018, 112)

Introduction

As noted in Chapter 1, there has been increasing interest in the idea of wellbeing as a goal of public policy. A range of economic and social challenges (Chapter 1) have prompted calls to refocus government action more directly on 'what matters' to citizens and the search for new ideas to address a sense that 'all is not well' (White 2017, 133). This search has led to new wellbeing measurement frameworks both within international organisations and in a diverse range of national contexts (below). At the most ambitious level, wellbeing is seen as an idea that could reorientate the overarching goals of public policy away from the dominant focus on economic goals, emblemised by the pursuit of Gross Domestic Product (GDP)[1] growth, which has long been taken as a proxy for social progress. For others, wellbeing can at least provide an important tool of policy analysis that might be used as an alternative (or complement to) more established techniques of neoclassical economics (below) and thus reorientate the focus of at least some policies.

This chapter introduces the idea of wellbeing, outlining some of the main philosophical contributions and how they relate to contemporary developments. It discusses the controversial notion of subjective wellbeing, which is seen to have a prominent place in UK policy thinking on wellbeing. The chapter provides an overview of key developments in the rise of wellbeing in politics and policy both internationally and within the UK, leading up to the creation of the What Works Centre for Wellbeing in 2015. It then turns to the role of wellbeing in policy, providing examples of evidence on how policies relate to different drivers of wellbeing and to a key indicator of subjective wellbeing: life satisfaction. The chapter concludes by drawing together some of the key themes and issues that inform subsequent chapters.

---

[1] Gross Domestic Product refers to the market value of goods produced within a country's borders. It succeeded GNP as the benchmark for economic growth in the early 1990s. GNP refers to the total market value of goods and services produced by the residents of a country, even if they are living abroad. GDP and GNP are alternative ways of measuring the same phenomenon and have subjected to same criticisms relating to the dominant focus on economic growth.

The Idea of Wellbeing

In common parlance, wellbeing is often taken as synonymous with the terms 'happiness' and 'quality of life', among others, but each has a particular meaning in the academic literature. Happiness is the most specific of these terms and usually refers to the experience of pleasure and the absence of pain. Wellbeing and quality of life are broader ideas that generally incorporate the notion of happiness but also relate to other qualities that contribute to notions of the good life and the good society. These issues are dealt with in more detail below, but at this point, it is important to signal that the focus on 'wellbeing' in this book reflects the dominant focus and terminology of UK policy debates. Specifically, in this book wellbeing is understood in terms defined by the Office for National Statistics (ONS) Measuring National Well-being programme. This covers personal wellbeing; our relationships; health; what we do (work and leisure); where we live; personal finance; economy; education and skills; governance; and environment (ONS 2019). However, at certain points of the book it is important to distinguish between different ideas—happiness and wellbeing in particular—because where they are used to have specific meanings this can have quite different connotations for both evidence and policy. Current debates on wellbeing draw on accounts of the good life that have their roots in ancient ethical theory that frame the ways in which wellbeing can and should be pursued, either by the individual, by society or by government. Of particular importance is the contrast between eudaimonic and hedonic conceptions of the good life.

Aristotle's concept of eudaimonia placed human flourishing as the purpose in life and one that was achievable through the continuous action and experience of living: 'doing' and 'being'. He postulates a perfectionist conception of what constitutes *eudaimonia* that is, put simply, the fulfilment of a person's highest human potential through the cultivation of a number of virtues, which include: courage, justice, moderation, honesty, greatness of soul, hospitality, cultivation of knowledge and perceptiveness, proper judgement and practical wisdom (Nussbaum 1993, 245–246; Bache and Scott 2018, 1–24). These virtues help to ensure 'appropriate functioning' in each sphere of life.

The Aristotelian tradition lives on in the contemporary work of Amartya Sen (e.g. 1985, 1993) and Martha Nussbaum (e.g. 1993, 2000), among others, whose 'capabilities approach' has been particularly influential in relation to development policy and its related measurement frameworks

(Scott 2012; McGregor 2018). This approach suggests that the sociopolitical objective should be the provision of conditions that allow people to develop the 'capability sets' through which they can achieve their full potential and find purpose in life. These capabilities include the provision of human needs such as education and health and, as such, this approach identifies an explicit role for government policy in promoting wellbeing. The capabilities approach shaped the development of the Human Development Index, which combines measures of GDP, life expectancy and education to compare countries the progress of developing countries (see Bache and Reardon 2016, 56–57). Sen was also one of the key authors of the 2009 CMEPSP report, which has been influential on many subsequent developments, including those in the UK (see below).

Classical hedonistic accounts date back to Aristippus and later to Epicurus, who developed the Epicurean school of philosophy, and place emphasis on the maximisation of pleasure and the freedom from pain. Hedonistic perspectives in contemporary wellbeing debates are closely associated with Utilitarianism (Bentham 1996 [1823]; Mill 2001 [1863]) and identify happiness—understood as the experience of pleasure and the absence of pain—as the ultimate goal. Thus, hedonistic accounts place the emphasis on personal feelings and experience and privilege the role of the individual in defining and attaining wellbeing. Bentham believed that the role of the state was to promote happiness through rewards and sanctions but not to seek to define how individuals take their pleasure.

This preference for focusing on the individual is pervasive within neoclassical economics, in which it is assumed that the individual will purchase or behave rationally in the pursuit of their own 'utility' or wellbeing. Thus, providing opportunities for individuals to participate in a free market would allow them to maximise their income and use that to satisfy their preferences. This emphasis on income relates to the focus on economic growth as the key to wellbeing and thus the emphasis on GDP. The hedonic tradition is also prominent in current wellbeing debates, with influential scholars such as Layard[2] (2005, 147) suggesting that 'happiness should become the goal of policy'.

---

[2] Richard Layard is not only a prominent scholar but also a key advocate of wellbeing in policy circles: a 'policy entrepreneur' (see Chapter 5). He is a member of the House of Lords, co-founder of the campaigning group Action for Happiness, a member of the All-Party Parliamentary Group on Wellbeing Economics, and a central figure in the What Works Centre for Wellbeing.

Subjective Wellbeing and Its Critics

Emerging from the hedonic tradition, the idea of subjective wellbeing (SWB) is viewed as gaining currency in UK policy circles and beyond (Austin 2016) and also within major international surveys such as the World Happiness Report (McGregor 2018). While linked to the hedonic tradition, it is considered 'rather more complex than happiness' (Phillips 2006, 18) and has been said to have three components that can be treated as separate items: pleasant affect, unpleasant affect and satisfaction (Diener and Lucas 1999; see also Chapter 4). Thus, SWB is generally measured in surveys that ask questions relating to happiness and life satisfaction (see below).

Because SWB accounts for peoples own evaluations of their lives, it is viewed by advocates as anti-paternalistic and democratic (Diener et al. 2009). It also has the advantage of being relatively easily measured and requiring relatively few questions (and thus resources) in comparison with more complex multidimensional assessments of wellbeing. It is also seen to provide a common unit of measurement to assess the effectiveness of different types of policy interventions: one that provides an alternative to the dominant cost–benefit analysis techniques of revealed and stated preferences that are derived from neoclassical economics (Dolan and Fujiwara 2012, 17).

Yet the use of SWB in policy is controversial. Austin (2016) referred to the dangers of 'happiness' becoming a hegemonic discourse within UK policy circles: one that allows policy attention to be focused on individual responsibility rather than addressing the underlying structural conditions that shape the wellbeing prospects of many (see also Scott 2012; White 2017). Thus, SWB is seen to oversimplify the complex notion of wellbeing and, in doing so, 'largely ducks the political issues that lie behind many of the current major global challenges' (McGregor 2018, 216).

The preference for SWB is in some cases ideological, following Bentham, but in others can be more pragmatic, because it is a relatively easy way to measure and present wellbeing: at its simplest, through a single number. Multidimensional frameworks, by contrast, require a dashboard of indicators that is more difficult to communicate. While the UK ONS takes a multidimensional approach to measurement, it is the prioritisation of the SWB component of this framework in policy discussions that has drawn attention and criticism in equal measure. We return to this issue in subsequent chapters.

THE RISE OF WELLBEING IN POLITICS AND POLICY

Current interest in wellbeing as a goal of public policy is part of the second of two 'waves' of political interest since the Second World War (Bache and Reardon 2013, 2016), both of which have critiqued GDP as the dominant indicator of societal progress and as an overarching goal of policy: a role for which it was never intended.[3] In the first wave, progressive political figures were prominent. US President Lyndon Johnson (1964) spoke of the 'great society' being one in which 'where men [sic] are more concerned with the quality of their goals than the quantity of their goods', while Presidential candidate Senator Robert Kennedy (1968) famously argued that GDP 'measures everything... except that which makes life worthwhile'. First wave developments led to the emergence of new social indicators, but their impact on politics and policy was limited before the political momentum was lost in the context of recession and leadership changes in key countries in the 1970s (Bache and Reardon 2016).

The second wave emerged in the 1990s, driven initially by environmental concerns but given further momentum by growing interest in personal wellbeing informed by influential research in the fields of economics, psychology and neuroscience. This second wave movement now embraces a range of concerns relating to happiness and mental wellbeing and a range of social causes. Unlike the first wave, which was focused mainly in advanced industrial nations, the reach of the second wave extends to developing countries (Boarini et al. 2014, 5). The broader nature of the second wave is reflected in the development of new measurement frameworks both within international organisations (including the EU, OECD and UN) as well as in a diverse range of national contexts (e.g. Australia, Canada, France, Ecuador, Germany, Mexico, Morocco, New Zealand and The Philippines) and at subnational level (including initiatives in China and the USA). One estimate in 2014 put the number of new initiatives at 160 (Allin and Hand 2014), but others have emerged since. These various initiatives often reflect different cultural, intellectual and political drivers and traditions (Bache and Scott 2018).

---

[3]The person most closely associated with the development and institutionalisation of GDP, Simon Kuznets (1934) stated that 'The welfare of a nation can scarcely be inferred from a measurement of national income'. Among its perceived shortcomings, GDP fails to record the distribution of economic benefits (inequality) and does not take into account the depletion of resources (sustainability).

In 2006, the OECD published the report *Alternative Measures of Well-Being* (Boarini et al. 2006), which argued for GDP to be complemented by other indicators. The findings of the report were discussed at the second OECD World Forum in 2007 in Istanbul, which attracted 1200 participants from 130 countries—an indication of the momentum building. At the end of the second forum, the OECD, the European Commission, the Organisation of the Islamic Conference, the United Nations, the *UN Development Programme* and the World Bank affirmed in a declaration their commitment to 'measuring and fostering the progress of societies in all dimensions, with the ultimate goal of improving policy making, democracy and citizens' wellbeing' (OECD 2007). As Allin (2016, 3) puts it: 'The declaration was important in affirming commitment not only to measuring but also to fostering the progress of societies in all dimensions. It also identified the ultimate goal as improving policy making democracy, and citizens' well-being'.

A key moment in second wave developments was the establishment of an international commission by President Sarkozy of France to investigate new ways of conceiving and measuring economic performance and social progress in the wake of the financial crisis. The report of this Commission (CMEPSP 2009), often referred to as the Stiglitz-Sen-Fitoussi[4] report, called for governments to adopt a multidimensional conception of progress that included a range of objective and subjective measures, including measures of subjective wellbeing. Sarkozy (2010, vii) argued (in the Foreword to the book version of the report): 'We will not change our behaviour unless we change the ways we measure our economic performance'. This report accelerated developments in a number of contexts, including the UK, and gave confidence to those who advocated the use of subjective wellbeing in policy.

At the global level, a number of UN resolutions on the wider measurement of progress paved the way for the Sustainable Development Goals agreed in 2015, which embrace a multidimensional conception of wellbeing:

---

[4]The *Commission on the Measurement of Economic Performance and Social Progress* was led by Nobel Prize winning economists Professor Joseph Stiglitz and Professor Amartya Sen as Chair and Chair Adviser, respectively, and Professor Jean-Paul Fitoussi as the Commission's coordinator.

> In these Goals and targets, we are setting out a supremely ambitious and transformational vision. We envisage a world free of poverty, hunger, disease and want, where all life can thrive. We envisage a world free of fear and violence. A world with universal literacy. A world with equitable and universal access to quality education at all levels, to health care and social protection, *where physical, mental and social well-being are assured.* (UN 2015, 1; italics added)

The UN's plan for action records a commitment by all Member States to develop broader measures of progress to complement GDP (UN 2015, para. 48). It was in the context of this initiative that a number of commentators suggested that, 'the chance to dethrone GDP is now in sight' (Costanza et al. 2014, 1).

UK Developments[5]

Partly in response to the Istanbul Declaration and related international activity, in 2007 the UK's ONS indicated its intention to elevate its analysis of societal wellbeing (Allin and Hand 2017, 6). Following the 2010 general election and the formation of a coalition government, the Budget statement of June 2010 announced that:

> The Government is committed to developing broader indicators of wellbeing and sustainability, with work currently underway to review how the Stiglitz, Sen and Fitoussi (aka CMEPSP) report should affect the sustainability and well-being indicators collected by Defra, and with the ONS and the Cabinet Office leading work on taking forward the report's agenda across the UK. (Her Majesty's Treasury 2010, 10)

A pivotal moment in UK developments came in November 2010 when Prime Minister David Cameron publicly endorsed the ONS Measuring National Well-being (MNW) programme. In launching the programme, Cameron (2010) stated that 'we will start measuring our progress as a country, not just by how our economy is growing, but by how our lives are improving; not just by our standard of living, but by our quality of life'. He

---

[5] As noted in Chapter 1, this book focuses on developments at UK government level. However, there have been significant developments in relation to wellbeing in the devolved jurisdictions of Scotland, Wales and Northern Ireland. These are discussed in Chapter 6.

argued that MNW programme would 'open up a debate about what really matters' and 'would help the government work out, with evidence, the best ways of trying to help improve people's wellbeing' (Cameron 2010).

The ONS subsequently conducted a public consultation on what domains and measures of wellbeing should be used for the programme. In response to this consultation, ten domains were decided upon in July 2012: individual wellbeing (later renamed 'personal wellbeing'); our relationships; health; what we do; where we live; personal finance; economy; education and skills; governance; and natural environment. Most of the data for these domains were already being collected by the ONS and was simply repackaged for the wellbeing framework. However, four new subjective wellbeing questions were added to national statistics to provide data for the individual wellbeing domain, and it was this move that attracted most attention. The four questions were: Overall, how satisfied are you with your life nowadays? Overall, how happy did you feel yesterday? Overall, how anxious did you feel yesterday? Overall, to what extent do you feel the things you do in your life are worthwhile? Each question is measured on a scale from 0 to 10.[6]

The ONS (2012, 36–37) highlighted three potential uses for its subjective wellbeing data: overall monitoring of national wellbeing; use in the policy-making process; and international comparisons.[7] It argued that that the large sample size in the survey would allow comparison of different groups within the population or between different areas within the UK, which could allow policies to be targeted towards those whose wellbeing would benefit most.

The first data from the programme were presented to government in 2012, and they have since been collected and reported on annually. In March 2014, the UK National Statistics Authority granted the ONS wellbeing statistics national statistics status, which means that they comply with a 'wide-ranging' code of practice and are 'readily accessible, produced

[6]The ONS later added a 'population mental well-being' measure to its personal wellbeing domain. This measure uses the Warwick-Edinburgh Mental Well-being Scale (WEMWBS) to assess mental wellbeing out of a total possible score of 35 (ONS 2018a), https://www.ons.gov.uk/peoplepopulationandcommunity/wellbeing/methodologies/personalwellbeingfrequentlyaskedquestions#what-measures-are-included-in-the-personal-well-being-domain-on-the-measuring-national-well-being-wheel.

[7]The ONS later added a fourth use: allowing individuals to make informed decisions about their lives (ONS 2018b).

according to sound methods and managed impartially and objectively in the public interest' (UK Statistical Authority 2014, 1).

The launch of the ONS programme was accompanied by a flurry of activity within Whitehall. Responsibility for wellbeing in Whitehall was shifted from Defra to the Cabinet Office, to provide a stronger cross-departmental focus. In addition, a Social Impacts Task Force was created consisting of analysts from across Whitehall and the devolved administrations to help take the work forward within government departments. In 2011, the Treasury updated its Green Book policy guidance to government departments to include subjective wellbeing analysis alongside the market-based approaches of stated preference and revealed preference for the valuation of non-market goods in policy appraisal[8] (Fujiwara and Campbell 2011, 57–58).

However, the government was clear that the ONS subjective wellbeing indicators were still in development and that 'we should not expect at this stage to have examples of major decisions that have been heavily influenced by wellbeing research' (HM Government 2013, para. 4). Yet it also suggested that it had put in place some 'new foundations' for instilling a wellbeing approach (HM Government 2013, para. 4). Among these new policy foundations were a number of new departmental surveys and narratives relating to wellbeing and examples of wellbeing emerging in policy appraisal and evaluations on these developments (see Bache and Reardon 2016, 72–80).

Despite these developments in measurement and the initial steps within government, significant policy change has yet to follow. Knowledge on measurement within government is not matched by understanding of what policies might enhance wellbeing, for whom, in what ways and by how much. Wellbeing remains an idea characterised by uncertainty, complexity and contestation. Long-standing philosophical debates reverberate within contemporary wellbeing developments, leading to dispute over how wellbeing should be defined and measured for public purposes and, indeed, whether wellbeing should in fact be a goal of public policy at all. While some suggest it should be the overarching goal of government, others consider it to be the responsibility of individuals. Moreover, for those who seek a more prominent role for wellbeing in public policy, there are often different priorities: some are most concerned with promoting mental

---

[8] In 2018, there was a fuller revision of the Green Book, which had implications for the role of wellbeing in policy appraisal and evaluation (see Chapter 6).

wellbeing (Layard 2005), others with greater equality (Wilkinson and Pickett 2009) and others still with environmental sustainability (Jackson 2011) and so on. Taken together, it has been suggested 'the diversity, volume and velocity in references to wellbeing suggest a cultural tide that sweeps together a range of different interests and agendas' (White 2015, 5). For these reasons, wellbeing has been described as a 'wicked problem' that combines complexity, uncertainty and divergence (Bache et al. 2016).

As was noted in Chapter 1, while wellbeing measurement has been described as 'an idea whose time had come', this is not the case in policy terms. Yet the idea of wellbeing as a goal of public policy remains an area of considerable interest both in the UK and beyond. In 2016, the Chief Statistician and Director of Statistics of the OECD stated that 'In almost all OECD countries nowadays, national statistical offices have started to include these measures in their surveys.... [we] need to go beyond measurement' (Durand 2016). Speaking at the same event as Durand, the Director of the UK's Behavioural Insights Team,[9] David Halpern (2016) stated: 'The real lacuna is around intervention studies... what can you do about it? There is a desperate need to collate and encourage intervention studies to see what could actually move the dial on'. In short, a key challenge is to understand and act on 'what works' for wellbeing in policy: the creation of the WWCW in 2015 was in response to this challenge.

The What Works Centre for Wellbeing

In October 2014, the coalition government announced that funding would be provided for the creation of an independent What Works Centre for Wellbeing. Funding for the Centre was confirmed after the 2015 general election,[10] which gave a strong signal of the government's continuing commitment to the issue and its continuing faith in the value of evidence in policy. The Centre was established in 2015, with 17 founding partners, including various government departments, Public Health England, the ONS, the Big Lottery Fund and the Economic and Social Research Council (ESRC). The WWCW aims to develop a 'strong and credible evidence base which will support these organisations to concentrate efforts on inter-

[9]The Behavioural Insights Team is a social purpose company jointly owned by the UK government. It seeks to shape public policy through drawing on the ideas from the behavioural science literature. It is often colloquially known as the 'nudge unit'.

[10]The election resulted in a majority Conservative government.

ventions that will have the biggest impact' on wellbeing (Cabinet Office 2015). On behalf of the Centre, the ESRC centre commissioned an initial research synthesis of 'what works' and secondary data analysis in three policy areas: community wellbeing; culture and sport; and employment and learning (areas that Whitehall departments had already shown interest in). The initial work would also focus on 'measuring, analysing data, definitions, and identifying areas for further research on wellbeing' (Cabinet Office 2015).

In comparison with other policy areas covered by What Works Centres (see Chapter 2), wellbeing is more recent to the policy agenda and is arguably subject to greater contestation over definition and measurement. An evaluation of the use of wellbeing powers in UK local government[11] found different interpretations and discourses of wellbeing across local authorities and 'little consistency' in understanding of the new powers: 'there was indeed no "single" problem of wellbeing but rather a range of ongoing problematisations, which varied according to the interpretations of different stakeholders' (Griggs and Howarth 2011, 221). Such conclusions are reflected in the wider literature on wellbeing (e.g. Phillips 2006; Scott 2012; Tomlinson and Kelly 2013; McGregor 2015; Seaford 2018; Wallace 2019) and conflict over the nature of the problem, and thus, the potential solutions have led to it being described as a quintessential 'wicked problem' (Bache et al. 2016).

However, the ESRC (2014, 4) provided a starting point for the WWCW on how wellbeing should be understood, drawing on the work of the ONS:

> Wellbeing, put simply, is about 'how we are doing' as individuals, communities and as a nation and how sustainable this is for the future. We define wellbeing as having 10 broad dimensions which have been shown to matter most to people in the UK as identified through a national debate...[see above]... Personal wellbeing is a particularly important dimension which we define as how satisfied we are with our lives, our sense that what we do in life is worthwhile, our day to day emotional experiences (happiness and anxiety) and our wider mental wellbeing.

---

[11]The Local Government Act 2000 gave local authorities the power to promote wellbeing in a 'broader and more innovative' way than had been implied by previous legislation (Communities and Local Government 2008, 1). However, the power tended to be used symbolically or as reassurance in the use of other powers and therefore did not lead to significant policy changes (Communities and Local Government 2008, 4–5).

This definition set out common ground for the different programmes in the WWCW but, as the ESRC acknowledged, would not resolve debate over definitional issues. The extent to which personal/subjective wellbeing should be emphasised remains a particularly contentious issue.

The newness of wellbeing onto the policy agenda means that much extant research has not been conducted with this definition in mind and, often, relevant research has wellbeing as a secondary or even tertiary outcome (ESRC 2014, 5). As such, part of the task of the WWCW is to address challenges such as 'as the ability to establish cause and effect from such evidence' (ESRC 2014, 5). In short, the accumulation and transmission of evidence on how policies can enhance wellbeing is seen as a crucial next step in bringing wellbeing more fully into policy.

Wellbeing and Policy

In its advice to government departments and other agencies, the WWCW (2018) identified a number of ways in which wellbeing might change the approach to policy: at the strategic level (defining the overall objective of improving people's lives/improving wellbeing); at the policy or project level (designing options that improve wellbeing, based on evidence; using evidence to achieve better outcomes, as wellbeing in turn improves productivity, health and pro-social behaviours); and in appraising options (considering the full potential wellbeing impacts; quantifying wellbeing impacts and monetising where possible; reflecting the wellbeing impacts on different groups). A wellbeing approach is said to understand policy impacts that may not have been previously considered by other approaches and also highlight the impact of policy on different groups. Evidence can help to estimate the potential scale of policy impacts and possibly quantify this impact by calculating the number of impacts x the length of time.

The WWCW paper gives a flavour of the types of evidence being collected and an indication of findings in relation to some of the drivers of wellbeing. A selection of these is summarised in Table 3.1.

The WWCW also summarised findings that quantify the effects of changes in key domains on life satisfaction, indicating the level of confidence in the effect and causality. Some illustrations are presented in Table 3.2.

As can be seen from Table 3.2, the levels of confidence across different findings vary significantly, although there is a consensus in some areas, not least those where a relationship with wellbeing would be widely expected

Table 3.1 Evidence on drivers of wellbeing

Drivers of wellbeing	What do we know? Examples
Health	
– Mental health	Mental health and physical health are strong predictors of wellbeing
– Physical health	Enough sleep, physical exercise, even eating more fruit and vegetables are shown to improve
– 'Healthy' choices	wellbeing
Personal finance	
– Income	Income has a big effect on wellbeing for people living in poverty. But as income increases, and covers
– Debt	basic needs, it becomes less important for improving our wellbeing
– Financial uncertainty	Wellbeing also depends on our income relative to others; i.e., it is more important that what we have
	is higher than or the same as that of others rather than the amount itself
	Being in debt can be stressful and debilitating and can have very negative effects on wellbeing, as can
	financial uncertainty
Education and skills	
– Education level	Higher levels of education tends to impact wellbeing through the impacts on job quality and
– Life skills, capabilities	comforts in life
	Some things that life skills bring are good (more income, more citizen participation), some are bad
	(higher expectations, more awareness of problems). Continued learning is associated with improved
	wellbeing
Relationships	
– Close relationships	Close relationships—with family members or friends—and having someone to rely on are very
– Loneliness	important for wellbeing. Having wider relationships in society can also make a difference—for
– Trust	example with neighbours you can talk to and trust
– Friendships, neighbourliness	

(continued)

Table 3.1 (continued)

Drivers of wellbeing	What do we know? Examples
What we do—and purpose – Employment – Good-quality jobs	On the whole, having a job is good for wellbeing. Being in a 'high-quality' job is even better. These tend to be jobs which provide people with things like job security, good relationships with colleagues and some control over how they work Wellbeing is lower where work demands are high without support or the ability to influence how this work should be carried out Wellbeing is also lower where the rewards are low in comparison with the effort which is put in. These rewards may be in the form of salary or 'intrinsic' motivations such as a feeling of helping others
Participation – Participating in arts, sports, music – A minimal degree of volunteering, altruism – Commuting time	Different activities can affect our wellbeing—from physical exercise to taking part in music or art. And how we feel when we do an activity also matters. For example, giving to others or learning something new can give us a sense of purpose, which has a positive effect on wellbeing. Some of these activities have a longer-term effect The impact an activity has can depend on how we do it and who with. For example, getting to know others better can have added benefits. Or for some people, doing an activity alone might be better Where we do our activities matters too. For example, being in nature can reduce stress. There is evidence showing that those with lower
Broader environment – Fear of crime/safety – Trust in people – Access and satisfaction with services, housing – Natural environment	Security is important for wellbeing, as are feelings of belonging Access to services which address needs are important for wellbeing—as is satisfaction with these services There is evidence of a causal link with (poorer) air quality and (lower) wellbeing. Casual evidence links accessing the natural environment and wellbeing, as well as even having a view of the natural environment. The wellbeing benefits of, e.g., sport activities can be increased through by taking place in the natural environment and/or a secure and supportive environment

(continued)

Table 3.1 (continued)

Drivers of wellbeing	What do we know? Examples
Autonomy and rights – Participation – Self-esteem, dignity – Fairness	The opportunity to participate and influence decisions which affect us has, unsurprisingly, a positive link with wellbeing, when it leads to decisions which better reflect needs. Participation by itself is more complex. Self-esteem and dignity are important aspects of wellbeing A sense of fairness in decisions which are taken (e.g. by government or in the workplace) is an important predictor of wellbeing

Adapted from WWCW (2018)

Table 3.2 Evidence on life satisfaction effects

Domain	Change	Effect on 0–10 life satisfaction	Dynamics	Confidence in effect and causality
Work	From employment to unemployment	−0.46 (UK) 0.71 (Ger)	Immediate effect higher, then reducing, but no long-term adaptation	High. Large effects found in longitudinal studies, cross sections, recession-related and employment shock-related (plant closures)
	From full-time employed to part-time employed wanting more hours	−0.174 (W. Europe)	Largely permanent. Particularly strong effect for men	Effect very robust in cross section and panels, but causality unclear
	Being in a white collar job (e.g. managers, officials, clerical or office workers) versus a blue collar job (e.g. construction, transport, farming)	~+0.80 (worldwide)	Unknown	Effect very robust in cross section and panels, but causality unclear
	From no commute to 1 hour car commute	−0.012 (UK) −0.151 (Ger)	Unknown	Low. Findings disputed and causality unclear No RCTs
Finances	Doubling of household income	+0.16 (UK) +0.5 (E-Ger)	Persistent effect with elation peak	High. Effect found in panels, cross sections, and shock-related (lotteries). Height disputed and income measurement problematic
Education	Extra year of compulsory education	−0.03 (UK)	Persistent effects	High for UK, since effect found from 1972 UK compulsory school changes. Marginal result also found in other Western countries

(continued)

Table 3.2 (continued)

Domain	Change	Effect on 0–10 life satisfaction	Dynamics	Confidence in effect and causality
Relationships	From single to partnered/married	+0.28 (UK) +0.1 (Ger)	Permanent effect with initial peak	High. Ubiquitous finding around the world
	From partnered to separated	−0.40 (UK)	High initial effect, then some adaptation	High as found everywhere, but most find new partners so don't stay separated. Lone men suffer more
Health	From healthy to poor physical health (self-rated)	−1.08 (UK) −0.96 (Ger)	Permanent effect, but initial peak as well	High as found everywhere, including due to health shocks
	From depression to full mental health (4 points on a 0–12 scale)	+0.71	Permanent, little evidence of a peak	High as found everywhere, including large clinical trials
Crime	A doubling of fear of crime	~−0.30 (Europe)	Unknown	Medium: panel data based, often replicated, but drivers of fear not exogenous
	Victim of violent crime	−0.396 (Australia)	Effect largely in first year	High, but specific: effects are for unanticipated events that were recorded
Environment	Increase of 10 in SO_2 ($\mu g/m^3$)	−0.08 (Ger)	Unknown	High: effects driven by unanticipated changes in power plant emissions due to policy
	Increase of 1 hectare of green space within 1 km around household	+0.0066 (Ger) ~+0.0031 (UK)	Seems permanent	Medium to high: panel data based but no clear-cut exogenous variation, similar results by studies in UK

Adapted from WWCW (2018)

(e.g. physical and mental health). In this sense, the evidence is likely to confirm what decision-makers already think they know. Where this kind of data might have more impact, however, is in identifying the challenges for particular groups (e.g. by age, gender, ethnicity or location) and designing policies in relation to those whose wellbeing is relatively low.

CONCLUSION

This chapter has introduced the idea of wellbeing, outlining some key themes and issues that recur at various points in the book. Wellbeing presents an idea that can operate at different levels of policy, from challenging the overarching goals to a more limited role in policy analysis. It has long been the topic of philosophical debate these debates feed into contemporary views on what constitutes wellbeing, how it should be measured and what role government might play in this. Subjective wellbeing is highlighted as a particular feature of UK policy debates, although suggestions of 'happiness' becoming a hegemonic discourse in UK policy debates on wellbeing should be treated with caution: not only is personal wellbeing only one domain of ten within the ONS framework, but this domain is addressed through four questions that include an evaluative component (life satisfaction) and a eudemonic component (worthwhileness). Moreover, where personal wellbeing is reduced to a single indicator for policy purposes, this tends to be on life satisfaction rather than happiness.

In short, the picture on measurement is far from straightforward and is complicated by other issues that emerge at different points in the book, including the tension in the choice between universal and local indicators.

The chapter reported that while measurement issues have firmly arrived on the UK government agenda through the ONS programme, significant policy developments have been slow to follow. For those closely involved in developments, this comes as no surprise: the ambition of refocusing policy towards wellbeing has always been understood as a long-term project by its advocates. One of the challenges facing this ambition has been access to relevant and high-quality evidence that might help take things forward. The creation of the WWCW in 2015 was a signal of the need for evidence and also of the government's continuing faith in the role of evidence in shaping policy. As the early reports of the WWCW indicate, the availability, the quality and confidence levels of evidence vary considerably. Moreover, the evidence available addresses different domains or conceptions of wellbeing or indeed other outcomes that may have only an indirect relation to wellbeing, however defined. Beyond the collation of relevant and high-quality evidence remain major challenges in using evidence to shape policy. We now turn to the first of two chapters that present the empirical findings on wellbeing.

REFERENCES

Allin, P. (2016). The Well-Being of Nations. In *Wiley StatsRef: Statistics Reference Online*, 1–6. https://doi.org/10.1002/9781118445112.Stat07996.

Allin, P., & Hand, D. (2014). *The Wellbeing of Nations: Meaning, Motive and Measurement*. London: Wiley.

Allin, P., & Hand, D. (2017). New Statistics for Old—Measuring the Wellbeing of the UK. *Journal of the Royal Statistical Society, 180*(Part 1), 1–22.

Austin, A. (2016). On Well-Being and Public Policy: Are We Capable of Questioning the Hegemony of Happiness? *Social Indicator Research, 127*(1), 123–138.

Bache, I., & Reardon, L. (2013). An Idea Whose Time Has Come? Explaining the Rise of Well-Being in British Politics. *Political Studies, 61*, 898–914.

Bache, I., & Reardon, L. (2016). *The Politics and Policy of Wellbeing: Understanding the Rise and Significance of a New Agenda*. Cheltenham: Edward Elgar.

Bache, I., Reardon, L., & Anand, P. (2016). Wellbeing as a Wicked Problem: Negotiating the Arguments for the Role of Government. *Journal of Happiness Studies, 17*(3), 893–912.

Bache, I., & Scott, K. (2018). Wellbeing in Politics and Policy. In I. Bache & K. Scott (Eds.), *The Politics of Wellbeing: Theory, Policy and Practice* (pp. 1–24). Cham: Palgrave Macmillan.

Bentham, J. (1996). *An Introduction to the Principles of Morals and Legislation* (J. H. Burns & H. L. A. Hart, Eds.). Oxford: Clarendon.

Boarini, R., Johansson, A., & d'Ercole, M. (2006). *Alternative Measures of Well-Being* (OECD Social, Employment and Migration Working Papers No. 33). OECD Publishing. https://doi.org/10.1787/713222332167.

Boarini, R., Kolev, A., & McGregor, J. A. (2014). *Measuring Wellbeing and Progress in Countries at Different Stages of Development: Towards a More Universal Conceptual Framework* (OECD Working Paper No. 325). OECD Publishing. https://doi.org/10.1787/5jxss4hv2d8n-en.

Cabinet Office. (2015). *Government Guidance—What Works Network*. https://www.gov.uk/guidance/what-works-network. Accessed 8 September 2015.

Cameron, D. (2010, November 25). *PM Speech on Well-Being*. Speech Given by the Prime Minister. London. http://www.number10.gov.uk/news/speeches-and-transcripts/2010/11/pm-speech-onwell-being-57569. Accessed 9 January 2011.

Communities and Local Government. (2008). *Practical Use of the Well-Being Power*. London: Communities and Local Government.

Costanza, R., Kubiszewski, I., Giovannini, E., Lovins, H., McGlade, J., Pickett, K., et al. (2014, January 15). Development: Time to Leave GDP Behind. *Nature*. http://www.nature.com/news/development-time-to-leave-gdp-behind-1.14499. Accessed 17 December 2015.

Diener, E., & Lucas, R. (1999). Personality and Subjective Well-Being. In D. Kahneman, E. Diener, & N. Schwarz (Eds.), *Well-Being: The Foundations of Hedonic Psychology*. New York: Russell Sage.

Diener, E., Lucas, R., Schimmack, U., & Helliwell, J. (2009). *Well-Being for Public Policy*. Oxford: Oxford University Press.

Dolan, P., & Fujiwara, D. (2012). *Valuing Adult Learning: Comparing Wellbeing Valuation to Contingent Valuation* (BIS Research Paper No. 85). London: Business Innovation and Skills.

Durand, M. (2016, December 12–13). *Subjective Well-Being over the Life Course: Evidence and Policy Implications*. Comments to Conference at the London School of Economics and Political Science.

ESRC. (2014). *What Works Centre for Wellbeing 2014/15: Common Specification*. Swindon: Economic and Social Research Council. www.esrc.ac.uk/_.../what-works-wellbeing-common-specification_tcm8. Accessed 4 September 2015.

Fujiwara, D., & Campbell, R. (2011). *Valuation Techniques for Social Cost-Benefit Analysis: Stated Preference, Revealed Preference and Subjective Well-Being Approaches: A Discussion of the Current Issues*. London: HM Treasury, DWP.

Griggs, S., & Howarth, D. (2011). Discourse and Practice: Using the Power of Well Being. *Evidence and Policy, 7*(2), 213–226.

Halpern, D. (2016, December 12–13). *Subjective Well-Being over the Life Course: Evidence and Policy Implications*. Comments to Conference at the London School of Economics and Political Science.

Her Majesty's Treasury. (2010). *Budget 2010 (HC61)*. London: Stationery Office.

HM Government. (2013). *Well-Being Evidence Submitted by the Government to the Environmental Audit Committee Well-Being Inquiry*. http://data.parliament.uk/writtenevidence/committeeevidence.svc/evidencedocument/environmental-audit-committee/wellbeing/written/1069.pdf. Accessed 17 December 2015.

Jackson, T. (2011). *Prosperity Without Growth*. Oxford: Earthscan.

Johnson, L. B. (1964, May 22). *The Great Society Speech*. Delivered at Ann Arbor, MI. http://www.emersonkent.com/speeches/the_great_society.htm. Accessed 17 December 2015.

Kennedy, R. F. (1968). *Remarks at the University of Kansas, 18 March 1968*. John F. Kennedy Presidential Library and Museum. http://www.jfklibrary.org/Research/Research-Aids/Ready-Reference/RFK-Speeches/Remarks-of-Robert-F-Kennedy-at-the-University-of-Kansas-March-18-1968.aspx. Accessed 17 December 2015.

Kuznets, S. (1934). GDP and Well-Being "Key Quotes". *Beyond GDP*. http://ec.europa.eu/environment/beyond_gdp/key_quotes_en.html. Accessed 17 December 2015.

Layard, R. (2005). *Happiness: Lessons from a New Science*. London: Allen Lane.

McGregor, J. A. (2015). *Global Initiatives in Measuring Human Wellbeing: Convergence and Difference* (CWiPP Working Paper No. 2). Sheffield: Centre for Wellbeing in Public Policy, University of Sheffield.

McGregor, J. A. (2018). Reconciling Universal Frameworks and Local Realities in Understanding and Measuring Wellbeing. In I. Bache & K. Scott (Eds.), *The Politics of Wellbeing: Theory, Policy and Practice* (pp. 197–224). Cham: Palgrave Macmillan.

Mill, J. S. (2001 [1863]). *Utilitarianism*. Indianapolis: Hackett.

Nussbaum, M. C. (1993). Non-relative Virtues: An Aristotelian Approach. In M. C. Nussbaum & A. Sen (Eds.), *The Quality of Life* (pp. 242–269). Oxford: Clarendon Press.

Nussbaum, M. C. (2000). *Women and Human Development: The Capabilities Approach*. Cambridge: Cambridge University Press.

ONS. (2012). *First ONS Annual Experimental Subjective Well-Being Results*. London: Office for National Statistics.

ONS. (2018a). *Personal Well-Being: Frequently Asked Questions*. https://www.ons.gov.uk/peoplepopulationandcommunity/wellbeing/methodologies/personalwellbeingfrequentlyaskedquestions#what-measures-are-included-in-the-personal-well-being-domain-on-the-measuring-national-well-being-dashboard. Accessed 6 November 2018.

ONS. (2018b). *Personal Well-Being in the UK QMI*. https://www.ons.gov.uk/.../wellbeing/methodologies/personalwellbeingintheukqmi/pdf. Accessed 7 July 2018.

ONS. (2019). *Measures of National Well-Being Dashboard*. https://www.ons.gov.uk/peoplepopulationandcommunity/wellbeing/articles/measuresofnationalwellbeingdashboard/2018-09-26. Accessed 22 February 2019.

Organisation for Economic Co-operation and Development (OECD). (2007). *OECD 2nd World Forum—Istanbul 2007: Measuring and Fostering the Progress of Societies*. http://www.oecd.org/site/worldforum06/. Accessed 17 December 2015.

Phillips, D. (2006). *Quality of Life*. London: Routledge.

Sarkozy, N. (2010). Foreword. In J. Stiglitz, A. Sen, & J. P. Fitoussi (Eds.), *Mismeasuring Our Lives: Why GDP Doesn't Add Up*. New York: New Press.

Scott, K. (2012). *Measuring Wellbeing: Towards Sustainability?*. Abingdon: Earthscan.

Seaford, C. (2018). Is Wellbeing a Useful Concept for Progressives? In I. Bache & K. Scott (Eds.), *The Politics of Wellbeing: Theory, Policy and Practice* (pp. 97–120). Cham: Palgrave Macmillan.

Sen, A. (1985). *Commodities and Capabilities*. Amsterdam: North Holland.

Sen, A. (1993). Capability and Well-Being. In M. Nussbaum & A. Sen (Eds.), *The Quality of Life* (pp. 30–53). Oxford: Clarendon Press.

Tomlinson, M., & Kelly, G. (2013). Is Everybody Happy? The Politics and Measurement of National Wellbeing. *Policy & Politics, 41*(2), 139–157.

UK Statistical Authority. (2014). *Assessment of Compliance with the Code of Practice for Official Statistics: Statistics on Personal Well-Being*. London: UK Statistics Authority.

UN. (2015). *Transforming Our World: The 2030 Agenda for Sustainable Development*. https://sustainabledevelopment.un.org/post2015/transformingourworld. Accessed 29 May 2018.

Wallace, J. (2019). *Wellbeing in Scotland: Reframing the Role of Government in Scotland, Wales and Northern Ireland*. London: Palgrave Macmillan.

White, S. (2015). Introduction: The Many Faces of Wellbeing. In S. White & C. Blackmore (Eds.), *Cultures of Wellbeing: Method, Place, Policy* (pp. 1–44). Basingstoke: Palgrave Macmillan.

White, S. (2017). Relational Wellbeing: Re-centring the Politics of Happiness, Policy and the Self. *Policy & Politics, 45*(2), 121–136.

Wilkinson, R., & Pickett, K. (2009). *The Spirit Level: Why Equality Is Better for Everyone*. London: Penguin.

WWCW. (2018). *Wellbeing in Policy Analysis*, Version March 2018. https://www.whatworkswellbeing.org/wp-content/uploads/2018/03/Overview-incorporating-wellbeing-in-policy-analysis-vMarch2018.pdf. Accessed 6 August 2018.

CHAPTER 4

'What Works' for Wellbeing?

Abstract This chapter focuses on 'what works' for wellbeing, presenting the findings of original research on the use of scientific evidence on well-being in policy. It considers the importance of evidence relative to other forms of knowledge—political, professional and experiential. It identifies the accumulation of evidence as an important next step for wellbeing in policy, with considerable demand for scientific evidence of different types and for a range of purposes. The findings suggest the need for a broad understanding of 'what works' beyond the rational-technical sense often employed to describe the work of What Works Centres and in the use of evidence more generally.

Keywords What works · Wellbeing · Evidence · What Works Centres

This chapter draws on material from Bache, I. (2018). How Does Evidence Matter? Understanding 'What Works' for Wellbeing. *Social Indicators Research.* https://doi.org/10.1007/s11205-018-1941-0.

53

It's what works in a particular point in time for someone, somewhere… It's a kind of a nebulous concept that should always be evolving and organic. (Interviewee #1)

Introduction

As noted in Chapter 1, the main aim of this book is to understand more about the role of scientific evidence in the process of agenda-setting. In this context, this chapter presents the findings of research exploring with policy-makers and stakeholders key issues in the use of scientific evidence in relation to wellbeing in public policy. The structure is informed by themes identified in Chapter 2 relating to the factors that constrain or facilitate the use of evidence. It highlights evidence as a specific form of (research-based) knowledge and considers the importance of this relative to other forms of knowledge: political, professional and experiential. The chapter begins by looking at how interviewees understood key terms and issues: specifically the idea of wellbeing and the notion of 'what works'. It then presents findings in relation to the four features of the evidence ecosystem before turning to consideration of other forms of knowledge, the challenge of wellbeing as a complex idea and what policy-makers and stakeholders want from the WWCW. Following the analysis of this data, the chapter compares the findings on wellbeing with those in other What Works Centre policy areas before the chapter concludes.

Understanding of Key Terms and Issues

There was a consensus among interviewees that wellbeing should be understood as a complex, multidimensional phenomenon: a reflection perhaps of their close connection to the issue and, as such, their knowledge of current thinking within the government and other key bodies. Typical comments included:

> It works at different levels. So, at an individual level it's about feeling good and functioning well. At a population level, it's about creating the conditions that allow and enable wellbeing in communities and neighbourhoods to flourish. And at a structural level, it's about removing any significant impediments and barriers, culturally and socially that may impact negatively on wellbeing. (Interviewee #5)

> It's about how the nation's doing, how communities are doing and how individuals are doing. (Interviewee #6)

> Social, economic and health - many things – and how you fit and in and relate to the community. (Interviewee #2)

This point was made clear when they gave their responses on how they thought others, who were less closely connected to the issue, see wellbeing, which was quite different. Conflation of the term wellbeing with happiness and health was the most common responses. For example:

> culturally, some commentators across the UK view wellbeing as something that's attributed to and in control by individuals... sometimes the media characterise wellbeing as happiness, which is extremely unhelpful. (Interviewee #5)

> I'm not sure they really know what it means. I think they think it means having people become happy. (Interviewee #10)

> I think people try and sometimes medicalise it a little bit. People associate it more with mental health rather than how you fit into your environment and you social environment and so on. (Interviewee #2)

> When I hear it used in policy forums, it's often used more with a health emphasis. (Interview #8)

> Professionals in different areas will give different definitions... You ask ten people, you get 11 different answers, essentially. (Interviewee #14)

The findings illustrate the complex and contested nature of wellbeing and the coexistence of both broad and narrow definitions in the policy process. The conflation of wellbeing and happiness is quite common in the UK, not least because of the novelty of subjective wellbeing within the Office for National Statistics (ONS) framework and the emphasis often placed on it in policy circles (Chapter 3). A common theme of the interviews was that these definitional issues remain important for understanding the role of evidence in policy, and these are discussed further below.

On the meaning of 'what works', interviewees tended to give responses that reflected the purpose of the What Works Centres: that it related to the use and standards of evidence. Typical responses were:

Identifying, based on evidence, what works and then doing something with that information so it leads to change. (Interviewee #7)

...proven interventions and approaches. (Interviewee #6)

...have evidence of some kind of attributable impact. (Interviewee #8)

In short, most responses reflected a rational-technical notion of what works, although it was clear from answers to other questions that interviewees were also very clear of the importance of a range of other factors influencing policy (below). One interviewee outside of government distinguished between 'what works' as it related to What Works Centres and 'what works' in a more general sense. In the former case, this was seen as closely associated with evidence 'but not just any standards of evidence, but standards of evidence which place a particular emphasis on experimental or quasi-experimental approaches', while the latter was a 'nebulous concept that should always be evolving and organic' (Interviewee #1) and more concerned with what works for whom, where, when and in what circumstances.

The Evidence Ecosystem

Evidence Sources Used

Interviewees reported using a wide range of evidence sources for various policy purposes, which are detailed in Table 4.1. While academic research was acknowledged to inform a number of evidence sources, there was a clear signal across organisations that academic papers are not usually used directly by policy-makers. This is partly because of the volume of academic research, which means it is often received through summaries by think tanks or via seminars or face-to-face presentations. Another common theme across organisations related to the focus of academic research, which was generally viewed as not directly relevant to the questions policy-makers are dealing with.

The wide range of sources reported may appear at odds with the presumption of evidence hierarchies (Chapter 2): interviewees tended to reject the idea of a strict hierarchy in principle, with one suggesting that 'If you have a hierarchy of evidence that puts certain types of evidence at the top, then that immediately narrows the amount of available evidence to you, doesn't it?' (Interviewee #1). However, alongside this generally held view

Table 4.1 Evidence sources used (in no particular order)

- Commissioned research and evaluations
- Randomised control trials
- Systemic/meta-reviews (e.g. Kings Fund/NICE/New Economics Foundation)
- Voluntary and community sector studies
- Grey literature
- Syntheses of academic literature (e.g. by think tanks, voluntary and community organisations)
- Participatory approaches
- Focus groups
- Online surveys
- In-house research
- Academic papers
- Evaluations
- Seminars
- Parliamentary events
- All-Party Parliamentary Groups
- Secondary datasets
- Government reports (e.g. Cabinet Office, Department for Work and Pensions)
- Government surveys (e.g. ONS)
- Legatum Institute
- Face-to-face presentations
- Internet
- OECD
- Roundtables
- Co-production

was acknowledgement of the need to draw on different types of evidence for different purposes. For example:

> I think it's important that the ecosystem of evidence is equally valued and equally mined but that when one is looking for some direct correlation between an input and an output that might be subject to slightly more rigorous scientific, methodological means. (Interviewee #5)

There was a clear sense across interviewees that government preferred particular types of evidence that tended to reflect the hierarchies discussed above. However, for other organisations, particularly within the voluntary and community sector and within some local councils, participatory approaches involving their communities and/or stakeholders provided an important source of legitimacy. In some cases, these types of approaches—such as co-production—were privileged over other forms of evidence because of the greater legitimacy they were seen to bring to organisations and their chosen course of action.

Transmission Lines

Evidence on wellbeing is drawn through a wide range of channels, which are detailed in Table 4.2. Here, there is some overlap with responses on evidence sources; seminars and face-to-face presentations, for example, were generally seen as both a source of evidence and a channel through which evidence is received. Again though, there is variation across different types of organisations in relation to some transmission lines. For public health bodies, for example, Public Health England was important in the transmission of evidence, holding a particular authority through its status as an executive agency of government. Similarly, NICE was widely recognised as an established and authoritative source on health-related wellbeing: a 'trusted brand'. Several organisations paid for sector-specific information bulletins and/or used sector-specific search engines, while most made use of the Internet for general searches or social media (particularly Twitter).

The range of transmission lines indicates something of the breadth and complexity of the idea of wellbeing. Bodies such as NICE and Public Health England were clearly more important to those organisations with a more medicalised conception of wellbeing, while the Legatum Institute's research (O'Donnell et al. 2014) appealed more to organisations that focused on subjective wellbeing.

Generally, interviewees emphasised the importance of professional networks and personal contacts: 'You have the right conversations to make sure you're not missing any tricks' (Interviewee #9). Being well connected in this way meant that individuals often did not have to seek out evidence but found it came to them. However, it was acknowledged that this could skew the evidence received. Such comments illustrate the precariousness of assumptions that policy-making is based on systematic consideration of the best evidence available.

Problems

Numerous problems with the use of evidence were identified on both the supply and demand side (see Table 4.3). These ranged from awareness that

Table 4.2	
Transmission lines (in no particular order)	• In-house research and light touch evaluation, literature reviews, evidence-gathering • Commissioned research • Academics • Professional networks • Wider sector networks • Policy advisory groups • Guidance from national bodies (e.g. Public Health England) • Circulars (NICE, National Health Service, Kings Fund, etc.) around specific issues, such as obesity • Twitter • Search engines (e.g. PubMed) • Conferences ('useful for finding out what's happening in other organisations') • 'People send us things' (e.g. emails from think tanks) • Meetings (e.g. with Alliance for Useful Evidence, NESTA) • Information services (i.e. regular bulletins) • Universities • Private consultancy organisations • Co-production • Presentations • Internet • Parliamentary events • Seminars • Legatum Institute

evidence exists, to being able to understand it. How evidence is presented is an important issue, with a number of interviewees commenting on the difficulty of understanding academic articles and emphasising the importance of 'plain English' and the need for 'a crisp summary and clear recommendations and sound methodology' (Interviewee #8). For most interviewees, not having direct access to academic papers through university libraries put a further barrier in the way: 'Unless I can download it instantly, print it off, have it there and make sure I've given some time to read it, it's no good to me' (Interviewee #9). This latter quote also highlights the common constraint of the limited time available to policy-makers to engage with academic research. In addition to the issue of time were shared challenges of timing and timeframes—for example, the mismatch between research timeframes and political cycles—which often led to sub-optimal outcomes.

Table 4.3 Problems with the use of evidence (in no particular order)

- Awareness ('knowing that it exists')
- Understanding evidence
- Understanding who the evidence is for and why they need it
- Lack of staff skill in using evidence
- Timeframes (i.e. within which impact has to be seen: 'It takes time to commission decent work and produce decent work')
- Timeliness (i.e. evidence not available when it is needed; legislative cycle not right)
- Time pressures (on staff)
- Funding/capacity constraints
- Access to evidence (e.g. academic journals)
- Policy-making is 'messy' (not rational and linear)
- Valuing evidence ('are policy-makers really willing to put some money behind generating new evidence?')
- Bad evidence
- Lack of clarity about where the evidence is coming from
- Academic work not accessible/practical ('think tanks put recommendations on first page')
- Lack of clarity on the relative strengths of the evidence
- Challenging the default position ('some are culturally and educationally programmed to consider only one type of evidence')
- Evidence focused on individual outcomes not social (e.g. 'improving blood pressure, not social capital')
- Qualitative evidence less valued
- Sheer volume of research
- Evidence contradicts the principle of co-production

A further issue related to the effects of public spending cuts on strategies for using evidence in policy. As one interviewee put it:

> It can take a generation to influence a community... but it is difficult to plan in advance with financial uncertainty. It stifles innovation and planning. You look for options that can give more immediate results. (Interviewee #2)

The quality of evidence was an important concern across organisations, with one interviewee stating 'I think there's a lot of really bad evidence that gives wellbeing a bad name out there... a woolly kind of perspective' (Interviewee #14). There was also common concern that the relative strength of the evidence available was often insufficiently clear. As one interviewee suggested:

> I think it is beholden in publications to say, "Look, this is what we're basing these findings or statements on and here's the levels of evidence". So it's just that much more honest and open, transparent way of which evidence is being used. And letting people make up their own mind to a certain extent. (Interviewee #5)

Finally, a number of interviewees pointed to the complexity or messiness of the policy process. As one UK civil servant put it:

> ...it's not [the case of] here's a problem, let's explore the problem, let's engage the public in a problem, let's look at the evidence, let's commission new research around it, and have lots of time to do all of this and make the best use of evidence that you can. Then come up with solutions, appraise the options, do all of that type of stuff. I don't think that happens very often. (Interviewee #6)

Interviewees across the board pointed to the importance of competing issues and interests, political commitments, public opinion and other forms of knowledge (see below). Such comments highlighted a general awareness of the need to understand 'what works' beyond the rational-technical sense of the term.

Incentives

A range of internal and external incentives for using evidence were reported (Table 4.4), again with some variation across organisations. For civil servants, there was an expectation that policies would be based on evidence:

> If you're publishing a policy you've got to back it with evidence... [There are] decision-making gates to get through for big policies, like impact assessments and business cases, spending reviews. So big incentives are built into the system in some respects. (Interviewee #6)

Civil servants also identified the importance of evidence in justifying policies to the public, which would be a consideration for politicians in particular.

Table 4.4 Incentives for the use of evidence (in no particular order)	• Quality of 'own' work • Assurance processes • Value for money • Population benefits • Producing better policies • Influencing government • To get more funding • To learn and improve • Credibility • Appraisal processes within Whitehall • Confidence

For charitable organisations, evidence was seen as important to their credibility. It might provide a 'seat at the table'. As one interviewee from this sector put it:

> it's even more important in the current climate in that there is a definite view that charities are kind of ideologically-driven, political mouthpieces… you leave yourself very, very vulnerable to [this criticism] if you're not evidence-based. (Interviewee #7)

Generally, interviewees from all organisations seeking to influence government acknowledged that sound evidence is essential. As one local government interviewee stated: 'We want this evidence to be so strong that the government and the Treasury cannot turn away the findings because they're methodologically unsound' (Interviewee #9). Concern with demonstrating value for money, which had intensified in the context of economic recession, was a key factor within all individual organisations and in the wider policy arena (see also Chapter 5).

Other Forms of Knowledge

While there was general acknowledgement that evidence can play an important role in policy, there was also general awareness that other forms of knowledge—political, professional and experiential (Chapter 2)—were also important: and in some cases, much more so. As one interviewee put it:

> People understand that the evidence ecosystem is pooled and shaped and manipulated in different directions by each of those different interests,

whether it's local advocacy, whether it's political advocacy, whether it's economic advocacy. (Interviewee #5)

Awareness of the importance of political knowledge was most prominent in the highly politicised environments of local and central government. One local government official highlighted the importance of political knowledge in the following way:

> ... about a third of it you go in with evidence but you've also got the political knowledge of - especially talking about councillors - what are their political parties? What wards are they representing? Particular issues in their ward? What sort of things they've funded or supported before? It's putting it through that template of politics with a small 'p' at the local level and all [of] your understanding [of] the structures that the council operates within. (Interviewee #2)

Another local government official (Interviewee #10) made this point even more forcefully: 'the political decision has much, much more power than everybody else. So, you know, I can do all this work and then if the political people don't like it, they can just stop it'. She also highlighted the challenge that wellbeing faced in such a politicised context, suggesting that to privilege (subjective) wellbeing measures (Chapter 3) above other kinds would mean a change in the 'entire culture of the council'. This point was echoed by a national civil servant:

> It's very difficult for politicians to talk about wellbeing because people feel that politically there's not demand to express things in that form. They will focus on, for the most part, much more concrete intermediate goals, like you know, how can you reduce unemployment? They tend not to think, fundamentally in terms of wellbeing, at the moment, and particularly in politics, people are afraid that they will be ridiculed for doing so. (Interviewee #4)

Experiential knowledge emerged as an important theme across organisations but was emphasised most by voluntary sector interviewees. Comments included:

> Experiential knowledge is really important... knowing the local market is increasingly important (Interviewee #7—voluntary sector)

> Service users... can throw up implementation issues. (interview #11—charitable organisation)

> We proceed on a case-by-case basis... stakeholder experience of the problem, frontline workers who are engaged in your policy or who could help to deliver solutions. (Interviewee #6—national civil servant)

One local authority official explained how her council emphasised the co-production of decisions with local residents and stakeholders: this was central to its philosophy as a cooperative council. This approach presented tensions with an evidence-based approach:

> One of the big problems that I face, at the moment, is that it [the idea of evidence-based policy] is constantly used by people saying to me or my colleagues [that] as long as it's got an evidence base then it's bound to work. And that is very, very frustrating because that's not the case and therefore what it means is that it contradicts [the principle of] co-production. (Interviewee #10)

One charitable organisation also emphasised participatory approaches to shaping policies more relevant to local needs. One project led to the development of an index to guide policy based on what local people saw as the most important things in their lives. Such approaches bring potential advantages in terms of organisational and policy legitimacy, but the interviewee suggested that this project 'probably has some gaps methodologically' that would make this approach less attractive in other contexts.

There was a consensus among interviewees that much policy-making depends heavily on *professional knowledge*. As noted above, evidence may not be available or, at least, available at the right time. In relation to a decision over whether to invest in a significant spending programme, one NDPB official stated: 'we've taken a punt on what we understand... we know that the evidence to prove that is limited. If I waited for the evidence base to prove it I wouldn't have taken the punt' (Interviewee #9). Individuals representing membership organisations highlighted the value of professional knowledge supplied by their constituent organisations, who were often consulted on key issues.

The Challenge of Wellbeing

As noted earlier, interviewees across all organisations believed the complex nature of wellbeing and contestation over definition and measurement presents a particular challenge for the use of evidence. As one interviewee put it:

> It does need to move us into areas of scientific inquiries that are much more integral or integrated across disciplines. And that challenges the way in which academia currently organises itself and scientific funding is currently distributed. (Interviewee #5)

There were differences between those who believe a broad range of wellbeing indicators are needed and others who think that subjective wellbeing indicators are a way forward, pragmatically at least. On this issue, there was no consistent pattern across organisations. So, on the one hand:

> They say we can't reduce wellbeing down to a couple of questions. No, you can't, but if you think that it's practical always putting 20 or 30 wellbeing questions into a survey - it's very naïve to think that's the case. You have to sacrifice yourself and basically, reduce or boil down to a few questions. (Interviewee #6)

And, on the other:

> the use of subjective wellbeing as a dominant measure is because we – a lot of people - are looking for simplistic answers to very complex questions… we need to balance that with much greater objectivity. (Interviewee #5)

However, there was also a common view across organisations that contestation over definition and measurement was to some extent inevitable and that, as one interviewee put it, 'There's no point in criticising anyone's approach on wellbeing because it has to be administration/context-specific' (Interviewee #11).

What Policy-Makers Want from the WWCW

There were plenty of suggestions on what the What Works Centre for Wellbeing and evidence providers generally might do to strengthen the role of evidence in policy. Inevitably, many of these responded to the list of problems identified above (see Table 4.5).

A common theme was the need for complex research to be translated into short and accessible information. A number of interviewees identified a rapid growth in research on wellbeing—an 'exponential curve'—but

Table 4.5 What policy-makers want from evidence providers (in no particular order)

- Provide information that is simple and short
- Prioritise thinking (i.e. provide a specific focus within wellbeing)
- Develop a strong brand for the WWCW (so that it can be trusted)
- Be collaborative (not least with 'people on the ground')
- Improve accessibility of evidence
- Improve availability of evidence
- Make sure evidence is relevant
- Promote different types of evidence sources
- Link with other What Works Centres (because of the multidimensional challenge)
- 'Share information and problem-solve about things that are happening'
- Scale up examples of good practice (e.g. within a community)
- Provide specialist knowledge and advice
- Build the capacity of organisations and people to do their own analysis and generate their own wellbeing evidence (particularly the voluntary and community sector)
- Address definitional issues and help to build consensus around the term 'wellbeing' and related metrics (e.g. in government)
- Find more innovative, creative and successful channels of evidence transmission
- Give evidence beyond what might be politically expedient at the time
- Create a demand for wellbeing information, evidence, knowledge, science and statistics
- Translate new law and policy (e.g. explain the political and legal levers and how that translates at the local level)
- Support small scale organisations/voluntary and community sector
- Provide an online resource bank for different methods/latest research
- Organise events
- Have direct contact with organisations
- Provide clarity around legitimacy given to different ideas of looking at wellbeing (e.g. 'subjective wellbeingsubjective wellbeing is only one way')
- Provide insight into upcoming/emerging trends on wellbeing
- Give 'concrete examples' about things that worked successfully
- Explain *why* something worked
- Provide examples of successful co-production

suggested that it has 'tended to be a very academic subject' that evidence providers need to 'convert into something that's very clearly actionable and can influence decisions' (Interviewee #6).

A number of interviewees also raised the issue of whether the WWCW should have a specific focus (e.g. mental wellbeing, subjective wellbeing). One gave the example of how the Joseph Rowntree Foundation had focused specifically on poverty and had developed a respected reputation on this issue. However, there was no clear consensus among interviewees on what this focus should be for the WWCW.

There was some consensus on the need to embrace and promote different types of evidence. One interviewee stated that the complexity of wellbeing required:

> ...a much more modern way of addressing the issues; a much more integrated sense of all of these things together. And that lends itself to, I think, new and potentially very exciting forms of evidence... the What Works Centre for Wellbeing needs to promulgate that ecosystem and multiplicity of what we consider as justifiable evidence. (Interviewee #5)

Another interviewee suggested that 'sometimes evidence gets used because it's the most visible' and the Centre should 'bring a lot more evidence into play to make that more visible' (Interviewee #5).

Finally, some interviewees believed the Centre might also play a key role over definitional issues and in promoting a 'common currency' for comparison of wellbeing interventions. However, while the ONS subjective wellbeing questions were seen as having the widest recognition in this regard, and for some were the best way forward (above), there was no consensus on this issue: other interviewees suggested that the WWCW should focus on setting out different measures for different purposes.

ANALYSIS

There was a consensus among interviewees that the accumulation of evidence is an important next step for wellbeing in policy. The interviewees indicated considerable demand for evidence of different types and for a range of purposes. While there are issues about definition and measurement outstanding, and an ongoing challenge to persuade key actors that this is an important policy issue, interviewees generally believed that scepticism around wellbeing had receded significantly in recent years. As one put it: 'I think people do understand that wellbeing is important... They don't think it's mad anymore to be measuring this. I think what they want is to do something about it' (Interviewee #6). Central to this purpose is a greater understanding of what policies can enhance wellbeing, for whom and by how much. On this issue, evidence is seen to have a crucial role to play.

As noted in Chapter 3, wellbeing can be considered an *inherently novel* policy field: one in which less is known about 'what works' in policy than in more established fields. In such cases, the networks are less well established and there are fewer 'trusted' brands' in terms of evidence providers: an issue the WWCW is intended to respond to. However, as wellbeing moves from an abstract idea to one that is being defined more precisely for use in policy it also demonstrates characteristics of a policy *in flux*. What counts as relevant evidence is strongly contested, and there are disputes over the basic theoretical approaches. Should, for example, wellbeing be conceived as individual wellbeing measured by subjective wellbeing indicators? Or should wellbeing be conceived as a multidimensional phenomenon in which subjective wellbeing indicators are placed alongside a raft of other, more objective indicators? The answer at this stage is not clear: while the ONS collects data across ten wide-ranging domains, there is also a push to privilege subjective wellbeing, which is controversial in some quarters (Chapter 3). As noted above, there is no consistent pattern of views across or within organisations on this issue. The interview responses on this issue were informed more by the particular views of individuals, shaped by their different theoretical perspectives and values.

Yet the WWCW has been encouraged to pay particular attention to subjective wellbeing: as a potential 'common currency' that would allow the effects on wellbeing of different policy interventions to be compared against the same standard more easily. This may have the effect of privileging certain types of evidence over others and may also discourage some organisations (and/or individuals) from engaging with the issue if this approach is not seen as legitimate. However, while this approach has been encouraged for the purposes of the WWCW, this is by no means the end of the matter. Indeed, while the ESRC identified personal wellbeing as a 'particularly important dimension', it also acknowledged that the ONS framework is broad and that some aspects of this framework would be emphasised more in some policy areas than others, and that other dimensions may also emerge (ESRC 2014, 4; see Chapter 3). In short, as Mulgan's arguments would suggest, in the field of wellbeing the questions are changing as well as the answers, and evidence—far from floating free—is being generated and accumulated in relation to different theories and concepts that frame wellbeing in different ways. As such, these theoretical issues are inseparable from the evidence and are the only way of making sense of it.

As discussed in the previous chapter, there is no easy separation of facts and values in the use of evidence and, while much of the language of 'what works' implies a rational, technical perspective, how evidence is communicated is crucial. This is not simply about clarity and sound methodology but also about understanding the audience and the context and tailoring the message accordingly. A common theme emerging from the interviews was that evidence serves very different purposes in different contexts and this shapes the nature of the evidence sought. Thus, civil servants and others seeking to demonstrate efficiency and value for money may be drawn more towards quantitative evidence, while organisations seeking different types of legitimacy may prefer participatory approaches.

Such findings highlight the usefulness of the distinction between different types of knowledge. Scientific evidence is an important form of knowledge, holding a particular status through its perceived neutrality, although, as the research here suggests, values and ideology are not only present in the demand-side world of politics but also in the epistemic communities that supply the evidence. As noted above, researchers adopt different theoretical perspectives on wellbeing that are informed by different value structures. These perspectives determine the 'facts' and the data collection methods that are seen as relevant. However, explicit consideration of political, professional and experiential forms of knowledge provides nuance to understanding the role of scientific evidence beyond the simple rational vs. political dichotomy.

Political knowledge draws attention to a range of factors—values, ideologies, manifesto commitments, electoral competition, party factions, interest group pressure, the media and public opinion, to name just some—that combine in the minds of political actors to provide a sense of what is politically feasible and what is politically desirable. So, on the one hand, the pursuit of wellbeing might be considered desirable, but not feasible for any of these reasons. On the other hand, it is plausible that at some future point the pursuit of wellbeing through policy may become politically feasible but is seen as undesirable because it conflicts with other goals deemed more desirable. These issues are more pronounced in the more politicised arenas of central and local government.

Professional knowledge is arguably dominant in much routine policy-making. While some public policy decisions are widely debated and various actors have a voice in the process, policy-making often takes place in the relatively closed confines of well-established policy communities. Policy communities tend to have embedded norms and practices that constrain the potential for new policy ideas to take hold. Policy specialists know best 'what works' in and for their respective communities, and this tends to provide a bias against abrupt shifts in direction. This does not mean that new ideas and new evidence cannot lead to significant change, but it does mean that they meet with an inbuilt tendency towards inertia when they arrive fresh at the table: a theme that emerged across organisations.

Experiential knowledge draws attention to the importance of end users, communities and residents' ideas about 'what works' for them. This approach to 'what works' eschews the search for a 'one size fits all' approach to defining, measuring and delivering policy for wellbeing. It may mean a trade-off between generating evidence through means conventionally viewed as more robust methodologically in favour of capturing the views of the specific target audience for policy. As noted above, such an approach offers legitimacy for the delivery organisation and, in theory, for the specific policy that emerges. It is an approach that has acknowledged limitations in terms of scalability, and is thus less attractive to large governmental units than smaller community-based organisations, but is one that nonetheless provides an alternative to established assumptions of what constitutes valid knowledge.

Wellbeing in Comparative Perspective

Chapter 2 introduced research undertaken by John Shepherd (2014) that covers the use of evidence in six What Works Centre policy areas: crime reduction; health and social care; education; early intervention; ageing better; and local economic growth. As Shepherd's four features of the evidence ecosystem informed part of the research design for the empirical material collected for this book, this provides the opportunity to compare the findings on wellbeing with these other policy areas. A summary of Shepherd's findings is set out in Table 4.6.

As might be expected, there is a high degree of similarity in the findings on wellbeing with other policy areas, but there are also some notable differences. Across all policy areas, there is a wide range of *evidence sources* used, including a mix of generic sources (e.g. Internet searches and social

Table 4.6 Summary of Shepherd's findings in the evidence ecosystem across six policy areas[a]

	Sources	Transmission lines	Problems	Incentives
Crime reduction	• Campbell Collaboration Crime and Justice Group • Universities • NICE • Internet searches • Force leads • College of policing • Other police forces • Community safety partnerships • Society for evidence-based policing	• Strategic command course • Chats with colleagues • Visits to initiatives • detected through 'police grapevine' or via Twitter • Meetings with force and ACPO crime leads • Association of Policy Commissioners • Police science inst. (Wales)	• Evidence wells are 'shallow' and 'dry' • RCT capacity is low • Academics don't understand issues • Academics not good at explaining • No police evaluation funding scheme • Offers 'lack of understanding of what evidence is' • Poor connectivity with academics	• Better force performance • New Society for Evidence-Based Policing and College of Policing provide incentives and encouragment • Fulfilling 'moral and public service obligations and knowing what the latest thinking is'
Health and social care	• Specialist journals • Royal colleges (e.g. Psychiatry, Surgeons) • International meetings • NICE • General medical journals • British National Formulary • Internet searches • Twitter, LinkedIn	• Hard copy and online articles • Small group discussions (some via royal colleges) • CCG commission teams	• Lack of contextual evidence • Health technology assessment appraisals 'not fit for purpose' • Products of Cochrane evidence reviews often seen as unstable • Information overload • Academic language • Status of evidence • Nursing research often too theoretical	• Location of a NICE unit in a royal college an 'in-built' incentive • Royal College of Surgeons Clinical Effectiveness Unit outcome data • Peer pressure • Competitiveness between clinicians • Quality outcome framework (gen. practice) • Value for money

(continued)

Table 4.6 (continued)

	Sources	Transmission lines	Problems	Incentives
Education	• In-service training days (often private sector-led) • Colleagues • Action research in own schools • Social media (especially Twitter) • Department for Education • Education Endowment Foundation • Association of Commissioners of Children's Services	• Other teachers • Heads use evidence from other schools • Poor heads/schools generally not well connected • Educational commissioners in local authorities have RAs	• Low-quality evidence • Not enough evidence • Low credibility of academics who produce the evidence ('not in the classroom' • Lack of funding for Inset days • Lack of context-specific evidence • Ofsted seen as a problem by some, as are edicts from government	• Improve skill set, quality of life and efficiency (teachers) • Improve school performance (heads) • Fear of punishment from poor results/Ofsted local authority reports commissioners) • Improve reputation of local authority and attract better recruits to teaching/LA

(continued)

Table 4.6 (continued)

	Sources	Transmission lines	Problems	Incentives
Early intervention	• UK social scientists/Universities • International research literature • Local Government Information Unit/local authorities/SOLACE/Inlogov • Dartington Trust • In-house policy teams • Twitter feeds—(esp. from govt. depts.) • Children and Young People Now • Institute for Research and Innovation in Social Sciences/Institute for Government/Institute for Education • Office of Public Management • Local family support services • Pakenham Project • Chance UK	• Paper reports on evidence from policy teams • Twitter • Local authority training courses • LinkedIn • Local meetings • Newsletters	• Much research is sociological criticism or too theoretical • Lack of an ESRC field trials unit or other evaluation expertise • Research findings often 'too complicated'/'too wide ranging' • Some international models don't fit UK context • Diverse nature of delivery by different groups/practitioners • Paucity of EEF-style guidance on cost-benefit and reliability • Access to academic journals • Lack of evidence for some	• Commissions feel that applying evidence makes a difference • Getting financial returns on investment • Seeing better outcomes • Meeting government statutory functions • Success in delivering integrated services • Freedom to act on evidence rather than having policy dictated • Freedom to withdraw funding from services not

(continued)

Table 4.6 (continued)

	Sources	Transmission lines	Problems	Incentives
	• Family Action • National Family Intervention Programme. • DCFS/Department of Health • LinkedIn • Early intervention websites • NHS England commissioners		government policy changes • Late intervention rather than early intervention culture • Low-quality training • Lack of reliable outcome measures for service impact • Little evidence reaching front line	adhering to evidence-based practice
Ageing better	• Action research (with home care staff) • Joseph Rowntree Foundation • Care Quality Commission • Social Care Institute of Excellence • Department of Health • Care home managers and care teams • Housing 21/Age UK • Alzheimer's Society • Universities	• My Home Life knowledge broker and facilitators • Local, face-to-face meetings	• Snowstorm of information, often unusual, too extensive, irrelevant or obvious • Some evidence lacks credibility (not involved service users) • 'Avalanche of information' hides useful evidence • Conferences expansive/need time off • Evidence doesn't reach frontline	• Knowing about the 'horrific' lives that older people often lead • Delivering government strategy (esp. PM's on dementia) • Difficult economic climate an incentive to adhere to evidence

(continued)

Table 4.6 (continued)

	Sources	Transmission lines	Problems	Incentives
Local econ. growth	• Local agencies' knowledge often institutional data • Local authority/Local Government Association reports • BIS reports • National Audit Office reports • LinkedIn • ONS data • Business sector groups (e.g. Housing Association, Chambers of Commerce) • Academic articles • Bank of England reports • Economists and consultants • Chief Economic Development Officers Network • Universities	• Email • Hard copy reports • Informal local telephone networks • A (low profile) LEP networks • In-house enterprise partnership teams • Local Government Chronicle • Municipal Journal • Local business newspapers	• Little awareness that experimental evidence on effectiveness might be useful (not just statistical data) • Few university, think tank or social media sources used • Few respondents know about relevant courses/CDP opportunities • Evaluations 'usually unsound' • Too few evidence champions • Standardisation of growth measures needed • LEP communications can be difficult • Researchers not connected 'on ground' • Unavailability of some evidence • Lack of evidence database • Government inconsistency in its choice of evidence to win funding	• To build business cases • For applications for City Deals • Strategic Economic Plans • ERDF, ESF and LEP funding • Ensuring best use of public money (linked to career progression for some) • Reducing the chances of 'doing the wrong thing'—leading to waste of public money, lack of growth, etc.

[a]Often the responses to the domains varied according to different actors or organisations (e.g. teachers vs. education commissioners) but for the sake of simplicity and space these distinctions are not generally made in the table

media) and policy-specific sources (e.g. Education Endowment Foundation, NICE and Royal Colleges). Beyond policy-specific evidence sources, one difference with wellbeing was the use of participatory approaches such as roundtables and co-production, which are not reported as significant in other areas. This reflects the preferences of particular institutions involved in wellbeing—particularly charitable organisations and some local authorities—who favour participatory approaches to developing an agreed conception of 'what matters' for their target groups. However, this may also be partly attributable to the idea of wellbeing as a relatively new idea in policy and one that still has to be explained and sold to particular audiences.

In relation to *transmission lines*, the importance of informal networks as transmission lines is evident across all policy areas, for example 'chats with colleagues' (crime reduction); 'other teachers' (education); local meetings (early intervention); informal local telephone networks (local economic growth); 'wider sector networks'; 'meetings'; and 'conferences' (wellbeing). This was clear in the interview material on wellbeing presented above and points to the random nature of some evidence transmission. As one interviewee (#8) put it: 'Is it too simple to say people email me with stuff that they think I should read?' While another stated: 'really it is the networks. Making sure I'm linked with the right experts… reports that might come my way as a result of that to be perfectly honest. Not very scientific at all' (Interviewee #9).

Many of the *problems* facing the use of evidence were also common across policy areas. These include: access to evidence; the lack of relevant or good-quality evidence; evidence not being well presented (e.g. 'academic language'); too much information ('evidence overload'); and the status of evidence being unclear. The most obvious difference relating to wellbeing is that the list of problems compared to incentives reported was longer for wellbeing than for the other policy areas. This was in large part due to the newness of the policy area and the unsettled nature of the field. Thus, challenges that had been to some extent resolved in other policy areas, such as the availability of relevant evidence, were still prominent for wellbeing. There was seen to be less evidence that focuses on wellbeing as a primary outcome than for other policy areas and fewer evidence providers with established reputations. More generally, the wellbeing policy networks were less well established, so issues of awareness of and access to evidence were likely to be greater. More specific to the wellbeing field, the interest in participatory approaches created the 'problem' of needing to challenge assumptions about what constitutes valid evidence.

In terms of incentives, a number of themes were again common across policy areas. Better organisational and/or individual performance were prominent, as were broader goals such as improved service delivery and improved outcomes for citizens. Value for money was also a common concern. On incentives, there were no major differences with wellbeing, although the theme of 'credibility' was not explicit in other cases. This may be because this is assumed to matter in responses relating to better performance and improved outcomes but may also again relate to the newness of the field of wellbeing in which some actors, particularly from the third sector, felt that having sound evidence was important to securing them 'a seat at the table' in the emerging policy networks.

What comes across in relation to all aspects of the evidence ecosystem is the relative complexity of wellbeing as a policy idea and the unsettled nature of the field. As discussed in Chapter 3, there is significant contestation over issues of definition and measurement, underpinned by different value sets that also inform views on the extent to which government should seek to address wellbeing through public policy. These issues are picked up again in the chapters that follow.

Conclusion

In the UK, wellbeing developments have reached the stage where the government has created a What Works Centre to bring together the available evidence on how different policies might enhance wellbeing as a step towards wellbeing progressing as a policy goal. The research presented here highlights an issue that is complex, relatively new to the policy agenda and one that has contestation at its heart. In such a context, understanding 'what works' is a major challenge.

There is widespread agreement among policy-makers that evidence matters, but it is far from clear what evidence matters when, for whom, in what ways and to what extent. To begin to form answers to these questions requires a broad conception of 'what works' that treats scientific evidence as one form of knowledge that interacts with other forms to shape policy. No one believes there is a 'magic bullet' that can resolve deeply held differences over the nature of wellbeing, how it should be defined and measured, and the extent to which governments should seek to promote it through policy. However, this chapter does highlight a shared understanding across organisations of the importance of different forms of knowledge—political, professional and experiential—that are essential to the notion of 'what works' in practice.

Beyond this shared understanding of the importance of factors other than evidence are common challenges relating to the use of evidence. Some of these challenges are well documented in research on other policy fields, while others are challenges more particular to an issue that is complex, contested and relatively new to the policy arena. Different actors and organisations seek different types of evidence according to the way in which they frame wellbeing and also according to how they derive their legitimacy. Not only there is no obvious resolution to disagreements over definition, measurement and methodology, but also there is even no consensus on whether resolution is desirable. Advocates of a greater role for wellbeing in policy viewed this as a long-term process that competing conceptions should not deter. Generally, the shared purpose is to shift the focus of public policy away from a narrow conception of 'what matters' to people that is dominated by economic concerns and indicators. Movement in this direction has taken place without wide consensus on definitional issues, albeit with limited policy implications to date, but enough to suggest that resolution of definitional issues may not be essential for further movement in this direction to take place (see Chapter 6). However, there is agreement that more, high-quality and accessible evidence will assist in this task: but most effectively when a broad understanding of the notion of 'what works' is more widely embraced. The next chapter highlights additional issues in the use of wellbeing evidence, drawing on the insights of the multiple streams approach.

REFERENCES

ESRC. (2014). *What Works Centre for Wellbeing 2014/15: Common Specification.* Swindon: Economic and Social Research Council. www.esrc.ac.uk/_.../what-works-wellbeing-common-specification_tcm8. Accessed 4 September 2015.

O'Donnell, G., Deaton, A., Durand, D. Halpern, D., & Layard, R. (2014). *Wellbeing and Policy.* Report Commissioned by the Legatum Institute.

Shepherd, J. (2014). *How to Achieve More Effective Services: The Evidence Ecosystem—Crime Reduction/Health and Social Care/Education/Early Interventions/Ageing Better/Local Economic Growth.* Cardiff University/ESRC What Works Network.

CHAPTER 5

Evidence in the Policy Stream: The Multiple Streams Approach

Abstract This chapter analyses the role of evidence in the policy stream as described in the multiple streams approach (MSA). It outlines the main features of the MSA before considering the role of scientific evidence in the problem stream. It then discusses in more detail the role of evidence in the policy stream, structuring the discussion around the criteria for survival of a policy idea set out in the MSA: technical feasibility, value acceptability, tolerable costs, public acquiescence and receptivity among elected decision-makers. The findings indicate that while evidence may have obvious relevance to some criteria for survival than for others, it plays a role across all of the criteria—some of which are more closely related than previously acknowledged.

Keywords Evidence · Multiple streams approach · Policy stream

INTRODUCTION

This chapter considers the role of evidence in the policy stream as described by the multiple streams approach (MSA). In doing so, it brings additional insights into the case of wellbeing, while the empirical findings also inform the MSA. It begins by summarising the main features of the MSA, identifying the major components and the value of a multi-level approach to

© The Author(s) 2020   79
I. Bache, *Evidence, Policy and Wellbeing*,
Wellbeing in Politics and Policy,
https://doi.org/10.1007/978-3-030-21376-3_5

agenda-setting. It then turns to the role of scientific evidence in the MSA, which features in the politics and problem streams as 'indicators' but is rather overlooked in the policy stream. It considers the role of wellbeing evidence in relation to problem definition before turning to a detailed discussion of its role in the policy stream, structuring the discussion around the MSA criteria for survival for policy ideas. The chapter concludes that scientific evidence can provide an important resource for policy entrepreneurs in helping them to demonstrate how an idea can meet the criteria for survival—criteria that overlap more than the MSA literature suggests.

THE MULTIPLE STREAMS APPROACH

As noted in the introductory chapter of this book, agenda-setting is arguably the most important stage of the policy process: one that shapes all subsequent stages from policy decision through to implementation and outcomes. As Howlett et al. (2009, 92) note, 'The manner and form in which problems are recognized, if they are recognized at all, are important determinants of whether, and how, they will ultimately be addressed by policy-makers'. At the core of studies of agenda-setting is a focus on the dynamics of how ideas get taken seriously by decision-makers or are ignored—'non-decisions' in Bachrach and Baratz's (1963) terms.

Kingdon's (2011) MSA has proved one of the most enduring contributions to policy theory. First published in 1984, Kingdon's book has informed numerous studies (see Chapter 1) and its main components have remained intact ever since. The MSA seeks to understand why some ideas receive serious attention from decision-makers while others do not. It identifies three distinct processes or 'streams' of activity relating to problems, policy and politics. Problems can press the political agenda through the occurrence of a crisis or high-profile 'focusing events' or less dramatically through a shift in respected indicators, although how problems are defined or 'framed' is generally crucial to whether governments seek to address them. Policies generally develop through the accumulation of knowledge by experts and their subsequent proposals. In the policy stream, there is often a lengthy period of 'softening up' and ideas must meet several criteria for survival. Political processes affect the agenda through shifts in public opinion, changes in government and similar dynamics.

These streams operate in relative isolation from each other but provide the greatest opportunity for an idea to be taken forward in policy when all three are connected, that is when a policy solution is connected to a defined public policy problem in politically propitious circumstances. 'Windows of opportunity' create the possibility for streams to be connected. These windows can open through events in either the political stream (e.g. a change of government or a shift in national mood) or the problem stream (e.g. a crisis or a shift in respected indicators highlighting an issue that needs attention). While the idea of streams provides the structural dimension to the MSA, agency is encapsulated by the idea of 'policy entrepreneurs'—individuals who invest their time and resources promoting their favoured policy ideas and who seek to connect the streams when a window is open. Policy entrepreneurs are 'the most important actors for understanding agenda-setting in the MSF' [multiple streams framework]' (Knaggård 2015, 450). Their success is said to depend on three factors: resources (e.g. time and money); access (to key decision-makers) and the strategies they employ (Jones et al. 2016, 16).

In developing the MSA, Bache and Reardon (2016) drew attention to the increasingly multi-level nature of much agenda-setting. Specifically, they argued that: policy streams coexist nationally and internationally and intersect at certain points through shared participants to provide a two-way flow of ideas; political authority and policy competence is often unsettled and contested between actors located at different levels of governance (e.g. international/national, national/subnational); and problems need to be framed at the appropriate territorial level (or levels) and issues of frame conflict are exacerbated in the context of multi-level governance as more actors and institutions with a wider range of interests and values compete to assert their definition of the problem (Table 5.1). This approach acknowledges the greater complexity of the policy environment for evidence (Chapter 2) since Kingdon's model was first developed in the 1980s.

As, Cairney and Jones (2016, 92) note, each of the major concepts of the MSA—the three streams, policy windows and policy entrepreneurs—has subcomponents that are worthy of detailed attention. Further, they suggest that MSA scholars should clearly specify these concepts, their components and related processes within their studies and signal 'how their findings and operationalizations might modify, affirm, improve, or otherwise alter existing MSA understandings' (Cairney and Jones 2016, 92). To this end, the discussion below focuses in most detail on the policy stream and its subcomponents—the area of the MSA where the role of scientific evidence is least developed, but where it is arguably as important as any other. Before turning to this discussion, the nature of evidence and its place in the MSA more generally is considered.

Table 5.1 A multi-level multiple streams approach

	Multiple streams approach (Kingdon)	Multi-level multiple streams approach
Analytical focus	Temporal alignment of streams	Temporal *and spatial* alignment of streams
Policy stream	Focus on knowledge accumulation within one system of governance (generally national)	Highlights that streams coexist nationally and internationally and can intersect through shared participants
Politics stream	Focus on a single location of political authority for relevant activities (generally national)	Emphasises that alignment of politics across different levels of governance is required for effective action
Problem stream	Focus on problem definition (framing) at one level or within a single system of governance (generally national)	Adds that frame conflicts are exacerbated in conditions of multi-level governance due to the wider range of actors and ideas, making successful problem framing more difficult
Policy entrepreneurs	Focus on their role in the temporal alignment of streams to explain an idea whose *time* has come	Highlights their role as 'venue shoppers' seeking to sell their idea of the problem in different arenas and seeking to promote both temporal and *spatial* alignment (an idea whose *time and place* has come)
Policy windows	Argues that the opening of a window in one policy area can increase the possibility of a window opening in related areas through spillover effects (*issue* spillover)	Adds that the opening of a policy window at one level of governance can increase the possibility of the opening of a window in the same policy area at another level of governance (*spatial* spillover)

Source Bache and Reardon (2016, 148)

Evidence in the MSA

In the foundational scholarship on the MSA, Kingdon (2011) does not refer specifically to 'evidence', but there are indirect references to its role in the problem stream and political stream. On the former, he refers to the importance of 'indicators' in problem recognition—they are important in demonstrating that there is a problem to which a solution can be attached. As such, developing indicators and getting decision-makers to pay attention to them can become 'major preoccupations' for those pressing for policy change (Kingdon 2011, 93). The importance of new indicators for well-being has been an important aspect of developments, and this is discussed further below. In the political stream, indicators (e.g. public opinion polls) can play a role in signalling shifts in the national mood, which can shape the context for agenda-setting.

Other than these references to indicators, little attention is given to scientific evidence in MSA scholarship, even though Kingdon (2011, 68) acknowledges that 'academics, researchers and consultants affect the [policy] alternatives more than the agenda and affect long-term directions'. Some MSA scholars refer to 'information' in a broad sense, with Zahariadis (2008, 515), for example, suggesting the need to distinguish 'between relevant and irrelevant information' in the process of problem definition (see also Chistopoulos 2006; Mintrom and Norman 2009). However, these scholars do not distinguish scientific evidence from other forms of knowledge (see Chapter 4).

There are very few exceptions to this broad treatment of 'information', and these are mostly recent. One relatively early exception is Weible (2008), who refers to 'expert-based information' playing a role in the policy stream (as well as the problem stream). However, he does not demonstrate this point empirically in relation to the MSA, focusing instead on the advocacy coalition framework. A second exception is Ritter et al. (2018) who employ the MSA alongside the advocacy coalition framework to examine the role of evidence, research and other types of knowledge in drug policy. However, of particular value for this study is Knaggård's (2015) focus on 'scientists' and 'scientific knowledge' in her discussion of problem brokers within the MSA framework.

For Knaggård (2015, 450), problem brokers are those who 'frame conditions as public problems and work to make policy makers accept these frames'. As such, they focus on making suggestions that something should be done, whereas policy entrepreneurs make suggestions for specific policies. Knaggård (2015, 456) suggests that while knowledge is one of three elements in problem framing, alongside values and emotions, it is a 'crucial part of almost all framing'. Moreover, while knowledge can come in various forms, scientific knowledge is seen as one of the most authoritative, drawing on the idea of science as 'neutral' and thus able to offer judgement between alternatives without partisanship (Knaggård 2015, 456). However, following Weiss, Majone and others (Chapter 2), Knaggård (2015, 456–457) acknowledges that knowledge alone is seldom sufficient to construct a persuasive frame: values are also important in highlighting 'why we should care', while emotions give frames a particular 'tone'.

While Kingdon (2011, 127) refers to the importance of the 'substance' of ideas, as well as political pressure, in moving some subjects into prominence, the idea of substance is not developed. It is argued here that scientific evidence can play an important role in giving ideas substance and, as such, is a potentially valuable resource for policy entrepreneurs pressing for change. Scientific evidence is particularly important where the target audience is civil servants, who have 'the prerequisites for understanding those types of arguments' (Knaggård 2015, 459–460) and who can have a significant impact on the development of policy alternatives (Kingdon 2011, 42). In this context, evidence can help push ideas onto the agenda by both demonstrating their effectiveness and legitimising political action (Boswell 2012).

In short, with the exception of indicators in the politics and problem streams, there is relatively little focus in the MSA literature on scientific evidence as a resource in agenda-setting, despite the important role that it has been seen to play in other stages of policy-making (GSRU 2007). 'Information' in a broad sense is widely acknowledged, but it is clear that in the case of wellbeing—and undoubtedly many others—policy-makers are asking for scientific evidence specifically. As such, evidence can play an important role not only in drawing attention to a problem or in highlighting a shift in public mood, but also in shaping the dynamics of the policy stream in which policy ideas are developed and taken forward.

The Policy Stream

Jones et al. (2016, 24) note that while the policy stream is regularly operationalised in studies using the MSA, its subcomponents are utilised infrequently and, they argue, 'identification of the subcomponents of the policy stream is perceived as largely unnecessary in terms of specifying and describing the policy stream'. This is not the case here: policy communities, softening up and the criteria for survival of a policy idea—key subcomponents of the policy stream—are taken as important theoretical building blocks to the MSA as a whole. The starting point for this discussion is with policy communities—the specialists in a given policy area, whether from inside government (civil servants, special advisors, etc.) or outside (academics, interest groups, think tanks, etc.).

For Kingdon (2011, 117), the policy community 'hums along on its own, independent of such political events as changes of administration and pressure from legislators' constituencies'. While policy specialists are affected by and react to events in the politics and problem streams, the forces that drive the different streams are different and each has a dynamic that is relatively independent. The policy stream is analogous to a 'primeval soup' in which the generation of policy ideas resembles a process of natural selection: many ideas float around, with some being quickly discarded while others survive—perhaps altered (Kingdon 2011, 118). However, ideas do not just float in this soup—they are also pushed by policy entrepreneurs who are keen to sell their definition of the problem and solution. These policy entrepreneurs can emerge from any number of locations—inside or outside of government, in elected or appointed positions, in interest groups, universities, research organisations and so on. Their defining characteristic 'is their willingness to invest their resources – time, energy, reputation, and sometimes money – in the hope of a future return' (Kingdon 2011, 121–122). It is notable for the argument developed here that Kingdon's list of resources available to policy entrepreneurs does not include scientific evidence nor does the meta-review of the MSA by Jones et al. (2016) (above) or other notable contributions (e.g. Cairney and Jones 2016; Howlett et al. 2016; Mintrom and Norman 2009).

Before new ideas are taken seriously, there is often a lengthy period of softening up, during which time policy entrepreneurs seek to persuade policy-makers to support and use their ideas. The idea of 'softening up' recognises that institutions are often resistant to change and that such a gestation period is necessary for new ideas to overcome institutional inertia. This softening-up process continues even when there is no clearly defined problem a policy idea might address or propitious political circumstances. Kingdon (2011) talks about the softening-up process as 'preparing the policy community for some future direction, even though no immediate result is evident' (pp. 129–130).

Once an idea has the attention of policy-makers, it has to meet a number of criteria to survive. *Technical feasibility* relates to the potential for a proposal to accomplish what policy-makers seek to accomplish and is often closely related to effective implementation: that is 'will it work'? *Value acceptability* refers to the compatibility of a policy idea with the values of specialists in the policy community. Here, Kingdon acknowledges the different ideological positions of different specialists and also variations in the extent to which different policy areas are affected by values, giving the example that health is more ideological than transport. *Tolerable costs* highlights the issue of budgetary constraints in developing and implementing new policy ideas. *Public acquiescence* may refer to either the public in a broad sense or a narrower set of the public who have a particular stake in an issue—or to both—and policy-makers will often take the views of elected politicians as indicative of or closely tied to public opinion. Lack of *receptivity among elected decision-makers* can lead to ideas being discarded when 'specialists cannot conceive of any plausible circumstances under which they could be approved by elected politicians and their appointees' (Kingdon 2011, 139).

In the case of wellbeing, the softening-up process has proceeded to the stage at which this idea is taken seriously by government actors and the focus of policy-makers now is on the search for evidence to demonstrate how this effectively be brought into policy. Over a long time period, the work of academics and scientists from a number of fields has played an important role in this softening-up process, from the social indicators movement in the 1960s (Chapter 3), to the breakthrough research by Easterlin (1973, 1974) in the 1970s on the relationship between income and happiness, environmental studies such as the Brundtland Report (UNCED 1987) in the 1980s, to later contributions on positive psychology (e.g. Seligman and Csikszentmihalyi) and the measurement of subjective wellbeing (e.g. Diener et al. 2009). There are many other contributions that might be mentioned (see Scott 2012; Bache and Reardon 2016). Evidence from such studies has sensitised decision-makers to the possibilities of wellbeing as a policy goal: an enlightenment effect in Weiss's (1979) terms (see Chapter 2). It has played an important role in the development of wellbeing indicators, and while the development and testing of new indicators continues, much of the focus of evidence generation and collation is now on 'what works' in policy terms for wellbeing.

As such, the discussion of evidence in the wellbeing policy stream is organised around the MSA criteria for survival. Before turning to this discussion, however, we reflect more briefly on the role of scientific evidence in relation to problem definition, which provides useful context to the more detailed consideration of policy stream issues.

Wellbeing: Evidence and Problem Definition

As noted above, in the problem stream the main role of evidence relates to the development of indicators that bring attention to a problem. Whether an issue (or 'condition' in MSA terms) becomes defined as a problem is then a matter of interpretation. While the importance of indicators in problem definition can lead to the adoption of indicators with 'serious deficiencies', Kingdon (2011, 93) suggests that the 'countable problem sometimes acquires a power of its own that is unmatched by problems that are less countable'. Once a condition is defined as a problem, indicators are then used to assess the scale of a problem and to understand changes in the magnitude of the problem.

The power of GDP growth as an indicator of progress illustrates this point well and is an important part of the background to rising interest in wellbeing. Here, the problem was identified as the need to resurrect war-torn economies in the 1940s and 1950s and thus the need to focus attention on economic output. GDP proved effective in this task. However, over time, GDP was taken as a proxy for social progress more broadly, thus acquiring power in relation to a purpose for which it was never intended. Despite challenges to the dominance of GDP growth as a measure of progress, beginning with the social indicators movement in the 1960s and the more recent proliferation of new wellbeing indicators, it retains its hegemonic status politics and policy (Chapter 3). In Kingdon's terms, it may be argued that the challenge posed by these alternatives is less effective because wellbeing thus far has proven 'less countable'.

Nonetheless, indicators have played an important role in drawing attention to the issue of wellbeing. It is no coincidence that statisticians and economists have been central to key developments, such as the international conference of statisticians convened in Istanbul in 2007 and, in particular, the economist-led Commission on the Measurement of Progress and Economic Performance (CMEPSP) in 2009 (Chapter 3). The Office for National Statistics (ONS) has played a key role in the UK as has the Statistics Directorate in the OECD and Eurostat in the European Union (Bache 2013). The various initiatives have refocused at least some attention towards wellbeing and the launch of the CMEPSP and its subsequent report can be viewed as a 'focusing event' in the problem stream (Bache and Reardon 2016, 52).

Yet, while the CMEPSP has been influential in a range of places, as Kingdon (2011, 96) notes, focusing events only rarely carry a subject to prominence by themselves: they need to be accompanied by something else already 'in the back of people's minds'. In this case, the broader context was the financial and economic crisis, which had intensified the search for new ways of doing things. For some at least, shortcomings in key indicators were part of the problem leading to the crisis. In 2009, President Sarkozy of France had stated that 'For years statistics have registered an increasingly strong economic growth as a victory over shortage until it emerged that this growth was destroying more than it was creating' (Sarkozy 2009). In a similar vein, Pier Carlo Padoan (2011), Deputy Secretary-General and Chief Economist of the OECD, later suggested that 'the crisis has not just highlighted areas where our statistical capacity remains deficient, but it has also undermined the confidence of people in markets, public policies, and official statistics'. In both cases, the solution proposed was the development of new statistics that would better reflect 'what matters' in people's lives, leading to the CMEPSP and OECD initiatives that provided significant momentum in a range of other contexts (Chapter 3). Yet, as noted above, for a condition to be perceived as a problem requires an interpretive element. Three factors come into play in this process: values, comparisons and categories (Kingdon 2011, 110).

The importance of *values* in the use of evidence is well understood in both the academic and practitioner-focused literatures on evidence and policy (Chapter 2). Kingdon (2011, 110) illustrates this point in relation to poverty: all may agree that some people live in poverty, but whether such a condition should be defined as a problem to be addressed by government action will depend on political values. Boulanger (2007, 16) makes a similar point in relation to unemployment, which can be framed as either an individual or collective problem. The case of wellbeing is very similar. While, for example, the evidence might point to some social groups having higher levels of wellbeing than others, the extent to which this is interpreted as a problem for government depends on whether wellbeing is considered sufficiently important and then where it is seen as an individual or collective responsibility.

The factor of *comparison* is clearly relevant to wellbeing measurement in terms of challenging the dominance of GDP. One of the reasons GDP is embedded is because it has been established as an international benchmark for several decades and allows governments to measure their progress in relative terms. As Kingdon (2011, 11) notes, in the USA 'The mere fact of being behind in "the greatest country on earth" is enough to constitute a problem for some people'. There is a clear implication here for wellbeing measurement: indicators that allow for international comparability may be crucial if they are to challenge GDP. An element of international comparison has already played a role in putting wellbeing measurement on the UK policy agenda. In 2010, David Cameron stated that he wanted Britain to be 'in the vanguard' of efforts around the world aiming to change the measures of progress, 'rather than just meekly following on behind' (Cameron 2010) and the ONS identified 'international comparisons' as one of the three potential uses of its wellbeing data.

A final point relating to the interpretation of problems concerns how *categorisation* defines our ways of looking at a problem. Kingdon (2011, 112) gives the example of transportation for disabled people: whether this was classified as a transportation issue or civil rights issue in the USA made a 'tremendous difference' to how it was viewed and the action that followed. As a complex and multidimensional issue, wellbeing does not comfortably fit into pre-existing categories, although some would prefer to interpret it to fit with established public policy categories—social, environmental, health and so on. Others would suggest the need to forge a new category for government attention—subjective wellbeing (Chapter 3). This categorisation issue is a central dilemma for wellbeing, which is far from resolved among advocates (Chapters 2 and 4). Multidimensional conceptions and frameworks are most prominent at national and international levels, which allows for interpretations of wellbeing that are compatible with a wide spectrum of values. A shift to a specific focus on subjective wellbeing would be more of a threat to particular value sets and vested interests, and as Kingdon (2011, 112) notes, 'politicians like to put off that day of reckoning as long as they can'. However, while multidimensional frameworks may have broader appeal, they are also more likely to fail to challenge the simple appeal in public arenas of the single-indicator GDP. This emphasises the point that how an issue is framed is thus central to its prospects in policy. We return to these issues in the next chapter.

Wellbeing: Evidence in the Policy Stream

As discussed in Chapter 4, interviewees for this book were in general agreement that accumulating evidence on how different policies relate to wellbeing is a necessary step for the idea to be taken more seriously by policy-makers. In relation to the MSA criteria for survival, the use of evidence to demonstrate the technical feasibility of policy is of most obvious relevance to moving an idea up the agenda, but evidence also relates to the other MSA criteria for survival. The next section highlights the kinds of issues raised by the different criteria and is followed by an analytical section that looks at the implications these have for the use of evidence. The material is presented in this way to help illustrate the connections between the issues raised by different criteria.

Technical Feasibility

Persuading decision-makers of the technical feasibility of wellbeing as a policy goal requires evidence that government policies can demonstrably enhance wellbeing. More specifically, the evidence needs to indicate whose wellbeing would be enhanced, in what ways, by how much and in what circumstances (Chapter 4). Despite long-standing interest in wellbeing in policy, the underlying evidence base in relation to these questions remains weak. Several interviewees spoke of the need for more 'concrete examples' to help persuade policy-makers, with one suggesting that 'I fall back on the same examples that I always give' (Interviewee #11) and another saying that the lack of concrete examples helped create a perception in some quarters that the idea of wellbeing in public policy is 'a bit fluffy' (Interviewee #10). On the particular challenge of understanding what policies might promote wellbeing, one policy practitioner stated: 'we just don't know how to do it, particularly with regard to the more complex interventions... what the levers are in terms of improving wellbeing' (Interviewee #2).

Interviewees were also clear that the challenge also related to communicating the technical feasibility of policy in ways that decision-makers would understand and could communicate to wider audiences. One interviewee presented the dilemma in the following way:

> It's harder for government ministers to stand up and communicate to the public that, for example, the Work Programme has improved x number of people's wellbeing. Whereas saying they've got this many people into work and these many people out of hospital - those sorts of measures are easier for them to understand, simpler to write into contracts, particularly for the public services, and easier to communicate to the public. There's quite a lot of sort of systemic things that would need to be overcome. (Interviewee #8)

This challenge is made more difficult by the relative complexity of the idea of wellbeing (Chapters 2 and 4). Interviewees contrasted the difference between demonstrating changes to wellbeing compared to more established metrics, such as hospital waiting lists or accident and emergency waiting times. This issue was compounded by tensions within the epistemic and policy communities on how wellbeing should be conceptualised and measured.

Value Acceptability

As it sits within UK policy circles, the idea of wellbeing is not strongly attached to the value structure of any particular ideology or party. It was closely associated with David Cameron as Prime Minister, but has advocates across the political spectrum, illustrated by the existence of an All-Party Parliamentary Group on Wellbeing Economics and two others that are closely linked.[1] However, particular conceptions of wellbeing are more closely related to particular sets of political values. For example, some equate wellbeing with individual happiness (or subjective wellbeing), and this is seen as primarily a personal responsibility (Chapter 3). In this view, generally associated with the political right, the role of government should be limited to helping people to find their own path to happiness. From the left, a focus on individual happiness may be viewed as a distraction from focusing on social goals seen as central to wellbeing, such as reducing inequality or promoting social cohesion. This requires a more interventionist government response (Seaford 2011).

As noted above, wellbeing as currently conceived in the ONS framework—as a multidimensional phenomenon that has ten dimensions and includes both subjective wellbeing and more objective social indicators—offers a broad church that can appeal across the political spectrum. However, the ESRC guidance to the WWCW, while acknowledging these ten dimensions, also suggests that 'personal wellbeing is a particularly important dimension' (Chapter 3): a nudge to a more individualised conception that can be measured with fewer indicators. As discussed in Chapter 4, for some interviewees the push for subjective wellbeing within policy is primarily a pragmatic strategy to get wellbeing on the 'first wrung of the ladder' in policy terms (Interviewee 6). However, there are

[1] One on *Arts, Health and Wellbeing* and another on *Mindfulness*.

ongoing 'frame conflicts' relating to this issue that are underpinned by different value structures.

A further aspect relating to value acceptability that emerged from the research related to bias in the demand for evidence of particular types (Chapter 4). Interviewees spoke of not only the need to provide good evidence but also 'how you try and marry up those who are culturally and educationally programmed to consider only one type of evidence' (Interview #5). Such biases emerged in the findings on other criteria for survival (below).

Tolerable Costs

The cost of policy interventions is a perennial concern, but one that is heightened in a context where 'austerity' is the watchword of the day. Thus, for the idea of wellbeing to be taken seriously by UK decision-makers, evidence of value for money is a key consideration. The importance of value for money came through strongly in interviews and, indeed, was made an explicit consideration for the evidence programme teams of the WWCW (Chapter 3). This consideration strengthened the demand for evidence of particular types. As one interviewee put it:

> Given that all things in the government at the moment are very much financially and economically driven ... the strongest evidence that we can use for our purposes is generally economic, quantitative evidence. So we would probably filter out a lot of well-meaning and perfectly valid pieces of qualitative work just because they don't meet the needs of the government officials who we're trying to lobby, who are generally thinking in terms of economic value for money business cases. (Interviewee #8)

In short, tolerable costs were a key concern that needed to be addressed by policy entrepreneurs in the policy stream and were central consideration in the accumulation of evidence for an idea relatively new to the policy arena.

Public Acquiescence

Wellbeing is, for the most part, a policy issue that remains under the public radar. There has been occasional media coverage—for example, when David Cameron publicly endorsed the ONS's MNW programme in 2010—and there was engagement with the public through hearings and surveys when the ONS subsequently developed its measures (Allin and Hand 2014). At this stage, however, there has been no sustained public debate and no policy proposals of enough significance to provoke a marked public response. The BBC journalist Evan Davies (2016) suggested that wellbeing was not an easy topic to communicate to the public. This was something that might be resolved through the development of clear policy proposals: 'It's quite abstract to most people... when you've got some policies, then we'll have something to point the camera at' (Davies 2016).

This lack of public awareness was identified by interviewees as an issue that would need to be addressed for significant policy change to occur:

> I think what we have to do in the wellbeing arena is create more public awareness and demand for this agenda so it's not just seen as some kind of fringe side show at the World Economic Forum or one of 50 areas of concern that the Pope has... You know, it's how do you land this stuff in mainstream politics? (Interviewee #5)

So, while it was deemed crucial for more evidence to be supplied to policy-makers, communication with the public was also an important issue, which would require evidence that could be easily translated into public narratives:

> ...part of what we need are narratives and stories that demonstrate what this actually looks like on the ground to people on the street. We're not there yet. The conversations are still a little bit too intellectual, still a little bit too academic. (Interviewee #5)

Receptivity from Elected Decision-Makers

While interviewees generally agreed that increasing the receptivity of elected decision-makers to the idea of wellbeing was a key issue, there were different views on the nature and extent of the challenge. As one interviewee quoted in the previous chapter suggested, it is often difficult for politicians to talk about wellbeing because there is no demand for them to express things in that form. The same interviewee suggested that talking about wellbeing might easily be ridiculed in the context of more pressing policy challenges relating to foreign affairs or the economy. However, other interviewees placed a different emphasis on the challenge of political receptivity, emphasising the role of evidence:

I think the evidence is a really critical part of it. I think people do understand that wellbeing is important ... what they want is to do something about it. If you're measuring stuff and it's shining a spotlight on kids' mental health or dissatisfaction in the workplace, which is affecting productivity or whatever it is, if you're shining a spotlight on it through wellbeing data, you really need to be coming up with approaches to tackle it. (Interviewee #6)

The arguments that apply to value acceptability among policy specialists (above) apply equally to politicians: evidence will not change deeply held values. Yet these actors address different audiences and are accountable to different constituencies, which can require different types of evidence. In particular, the more public role of politicians places emphasis on policy ideas that can be clearly communicated; again, this is related to the idea of public acquiescence. As one interviewee put it:

I think there is a risk that the politicians won't stay the course with it if they don't get that bit of evidence ... it just needs something really high quality now, for people to be able to hold it up and say "this is the point". (Interviewee #11)

Analysis

As Boswell (see Chapter 2) has argued, the use of evidence depends on both the way in which policy-makers derive legitimacy and the extent to which evidence is viewed as a means of securing this legitimacy. This chapter emphasises the point that civil servants view scientific knowledge as a central component of their legitimacy and are ready to embrace relevant and high-quality research. As such, scientific evidence offers a resource to policy entrepreneurs, who can use the authority it offers to strengthen the validity of their claims within the policy stream: an argument that echoes that of Knaggård (2015) in relation to problem brokers' use of evidence in the process of problem definition. Moreover, the findings indicate that while evidence may have more obvious relevance to some criteria for survival than for others, it plays a role across all of the criteria—some of which are more closely related than previously acknowledged.

On technical feasibility, there was a clear instrumental demand for evidence to provide 'concrete examples' of how policies aimed at enhancing wellbeing can achieve what is intended. Part of this demand was the need for the technical feasibility of policy to be communicated in ways that policy-makers clearly understood and could communicate to wider audiences, including politicians. The research also signalled the importance of clear indicators of policy effectiveness in this stream—thus far, indicators feature in the MSA only as a means of drawing attention to an issue in the problem stream or in highlighting shifts in national mood in the political stream. Moreover, concerns with the complexity and communication of policy ideas overlap with the criterion of public acquiescence and may point to the demand for evidence of particular types.

While Kingdon makes a distinction between policy areas that are more or less ideological, the research on value acceptability shows that this does not account for policy areas that are not settled and thus their ideological content is unclear. This is the case for wellbeing. At this early stage, the nature of the evidence selected plays an important role in framing the idea, which is relatively new to the policy stream and remains variously defined. If the evidence made available to government privileges one conception of wellbeing over others, issues of value acceptability are likely to become more pronounced as it becomes clearer whose values are most challenged. As wellbeing becomes more tightly defined for policy purposes, this situation is likely to arise. This may be either because the evidence selected reflects the values of a particular coalition within the epistemic community or simply through a process of simplification as research moves from the wider community of scholars to those involved in summarising and interpreting for government. As Botterill and Hindmoor (2012) have suggested, bounded rationality applies to actors on both the supply and demand sides of the relationship. It may be for this reason that subjective wellbeing is gaining currency in the UK: that is, not through ideological preference but because it can be measured through a single indicator (e.g. on satisfaction with life), which is more demonstrable and more easily communicated than a complex dashboard of subjective and objective social indicators.

A further twist to Kingdon's notion of value acceptability revealed by this research is that it does not just relate to the policy idea itself but also to how different types of evidence are valued in demonstrating the efficacy of the idea. The evidence and policy literature draws attention to how forms of evidence are often placed in a hierarchy based on study design (Chapter 2). In the research for this book, interviewees identified a strong bias within government for quantitative evidence: a bias that had been strengthened in the context of austerity. In short, when examined in relation to the case of wellbeing, the idea of value acceptability reveals a degree of complexity and nuance not acknowledged in the foundational literature on the policy stream.

The criterion of tolerable costs plays a key part in shaping the prospects for an idea's survival in the current economic climate. This criterion increases the demand for evidence, but also of particular types. It demands evidence that factors in value for money and also contributes to a climate in which quantitative evidence is preferred by decision-makers. In the evidence-gathering processes, the distinction between technical feasibility and value for money is blurred as the latter is incorporated into the search for politically feasible policy options.

The criterion of public acquiescence provides another example of the unclear boundaries between criteria. Considerations of technical feasibility include the need to communicate policy ideas to wider audiences. While this may lead to the search for simple metrics, it may also require the search to extend to the construction of narratives and stories that are appealing to the wider public. This in turn links to political receptivity: politicians demand evidence-based narratives that will allow them to sell new ideas. This is particularly true in complex policy areas such as wellbeing that have to compete for political space with more established policy areas where narratives are established, for example relating to the importance of economic growth, and where there are recognised indicators to point to, such as GDP. This is not to say that other policy areas competing in the same space are not complex—GDP is far from a simple construct—but rather that a narrative has been established about why growth should be prioritised and GDP widely accepted as way of measuring policy success or failure. As one interviewee put it: 'particularly in an area which is sort of paradigm-challenging and a little bit different we need to have quite strong evidential base to help move people from their prior conceptions' (Interviewee #5).

Conclusion

This chapter has sought to contribute to understanding of the role of scientific evidence in the process of agenda-setting and, in doing so, to respond to the challenge of developing the MSA. In doing so, it has brought together new empirical findings on wellbeing to reflect on the dynamics of the policy stream and, in particular, the criteria for survival faced by new policy ideas. The findings indicate awareness that evidence can be an important resource for policy entrepreneurs in helping them to demonstrate how the idea of wellbeing can meet the criteria for survival. As such, the survival prospects of new policy ideas may be shaped not only by the existing criteria for survival—which overlap more than the MSA literature suggests—but also by the availability, nature and quality of evidence and how it is mobilised by policy entrepreneurs. In this way, evidence has a potentially important role to play in policy entrepreneurs coupling the streams and moving a policy idea forward. As such, while there are many other factors that influence stream coupling, the effective mobilisation of scientific evidence may prove to be a necessary prerequisite for success. The concluding chapter picks up this theme, along with others raised in this chapter, including the importance of a multi-level understanding of agenda-setting.

References

Allin, P., & Hand, D. (2014). *The Wellbeing of Nations: Meaning, Motive and Measurement*. London: Wiley.

Bache, I. (2013). Measuring Quality of Life for Public Policy: An Idea Whose Time Has Come? Agenda-Setting Dynamics in the European Union. *Journal of European Public Policy, 20*(1), 21–38.

Bache, I., & Reardon, L. (2016). *The Politics and Policy of Wellbeing: Understanding the Rise and Significance of a New Agenda*. Cheltenham: Edward Elgar.

Bachrach, P., & Baratz, M. (1963). Decisions and Non-decisions: An Analytical Framework. *American Political Science Review, 57*(3), 632–642.

Boswell, C. (2012). *The Political Uses of Expert Knowledge: Immigration Policy and Social Research*. Cambridge: Cambridge University Press.

Botterill, L., & Hindmoor, A. (2012). Turtles All the Way Down: Bounded Rationality in an Evidence-Based Age. *Policy Studies, 33*(5), 367–379.

Boulanger, P. (2007). Political Uses of Social Indicators: Overview and Application to Sustainable Development Indicators. *International Journal of Sustainable Development, 10*(1–2), 14–32.

Cairney, P., & Jones, M. (2016). Kingdon's Multiple Streams Approach: What Is the Empirical Impact of This Universal Theory? *The Policy Studies Journal, 44*(1), 37–58.

Cameron, D. (2010, November 25). *PM Speech on Well-Being*. Speech Given by the Prime Minister. London. http://www.number10.gov.uk/news/speeches-and-transcripts/2010/11/pm-speech-onwell-being-57569. Accessed 9 January 2011.

Christopoulos, D. (2006). Relational Attributes of Political Entrepreneurs: A Network Perspective. *Journal of European Public Policy, 13*(5), 757–778.

Davies, E. (2016, December 12–13). *Subjective Well-Being over the Life Course: Evidence and Policy Implications*. Comments to Conference at London School of Economics and Political Science.

Diener, E., Lucas, R., Schimmack, U., & Helliwell, J. (2009). *Well-Being for Public Policy*. Oxford: Oxford University Press.

Easterlin, R. (1973). Does Money Buy Happiness? *The Public Interest, 30*(Winter), 3–10.

Easterlin, R. (1974). Does Economic Growth Improve the Human Lot? Some Empirical Evidence. In P. A. David & M. W. Reder (Eds.), *Nations and Households in Economic Growth: Essays in Honor of Moses Abramovitz* (pp. 89–125). New York: Academic Press.

GSRU. (2007). *Analysis for Policy: Evidence-Based Policy in Practice*. London: Government, Social Research Unit, HM Treasury.

Howlett, M., McConnell, A., & Perl, A. (2016). Moving Policy Theory Forward: Connecting Multiple Stream and Advocacy Coalition Frameworks to Policy Cycle Models of Analysis. *Australian Journal of Public Administration, 76*(1), 65–79. https://doi.org/10.1111/1467-8500.12191.

Howlett, M., Ramesh, M., & Perl, A. (2009). *Studying Public Policy: Policy Cycles and Policy Subsystems* (3rd ed.). Oxford: Oxford University Press.

Jones, M. D., Peterson, H. L., Pierce, J. J., Herweg, N., Bernal, A., Raney, H. L., et al. (2016). A River Runs Through It: A Multiple Streams Meta-Review. *The Policy Studies Journal, 44*(1), 13–36.

Kingdon, J. (2011). *Agendas, Alternatives, and Public Policies* (4th ed.). London: HarperCollins.

Knaggård, Å. (2015). The Multiple Streams Framework and the Problem Broker. *European Journal of Political Research, 54*, 450–465.

Mintrom, M., & Norman, P. (2009). Policy Entrepreneurship and Policy Change. *The Policy Studies Journal, 37*(4), 649–667.

Padoan, P. C. (2011). *Statistics for Policymaking: Europe 2020*. Conference, Brussels, 10–11 March 2001.

Ritter, A., Hughes, C., Lancaster, K., & Hoppe, R. (2018). Using the Advocacy Coalition Framework and Multiple Streams Policy Theories to Examine the Role of Evidence, Research and Other Types of Knowledge in Drug Policy. *Addiction*. https://doi.org/10.1111/add.14197.

Sarkozy, N. (2009). Quoted in Davies, L. (2009, September 14). Sarkozy Attacks Focus on Economic Growth. *The Guardian*. http://www.theguardian.com/business/2009/sep/14/sarkozy-attacks-gdp-focus. Accessed 17 December 2015.

Scott, K. (2012). *Measuring Wellbeing: Towards Sustainability?* Abingdon: Earthscan.

Seaford, C. (Ed.). (2011). *The Practical Politics of Wellbeing*. London: New Economics Foundation.

UNCED. (1987). *Our Common Future. Report of the World Commission on Environment and Development*. New York: United Nations.

Weible, C. (2008). Expert-Based Information and Policy Subsystems: A Review and Synthesis. *The Policy Studies Journal, 36*(4), 615–635.

Weiss, C. (1979, September–October). The Many Meanings of Research Utilization. *Public Administration Review, 39*, 426–431.

Zahariadis, N. (2008). Ambiguity and Choice in European Public Policy. *Journal of European Public Policy, 15*(4), 514–530.

CHAPTER 6

Conclusion

Abstract This chapter draws the book to its conclusion. It recaps the main findings and reflects on each of the three main aims of the book. In doing so, it considers the political appeal of wellbeing, the importance of how evidence is communicated and the ongoing challenges brought by the complex and contested nature of wellbeing. It also considers the significance of recent wellbeing initiatives internationally and nationally, including those in the devolved jurisdictions of Scotland, Wales and Northern Ireland.

Keywords Wellbeing · Evidence · Scotland · Wales · Northern Ireland

Perfect is the enemy of the good. (Voltaire)

INTRODUCTION

The idea of wellbeing has been on the UK government's agenda for several years. However, while the measurement of wellbeing has moved forward decisively, significant policy action has not yet followed. The role of scientific evidence has been seen as a crucial next step in taking wellbeing forward in policy. In this context, this book has provided a theoretically informed account of the role of evidence in shaping the prospects for well-

© The Author(s) 2020   101
I. Bache, *Evidence, Policy and Wellbeing*,
Wellbeing in Politics and Policy,
https://doi.org/10.1007/978-3-030-21376-3_6

being in UK policy, from the *governmental agenda* to the *decision agenda* (see Chapter 1). The opening chapter set out three specific aims:

1. To understand the role of evidence in shaping the prospects for well-being in public policy.
2. To inform the multiple streams approach (MSA) to agenda-setting.
3. To inform the barriers literature on the use of evidence in policy.

This chapter briefly recaps the coverage of the book before addressing each of these aims in turn.

Chapter 2 considered the evidence and policy relationship. It identified scientific evidence as having a particular status among forms of knowledge as the 'dominant language of legitimation and persuasion' in modern societies and distinguished this from political, professional and experiential forms of knowledge, each of which plays role in the policy process. It unpacked the notion of 'policy', distinguishing between different levels, types and fields, before discussing the intensification of the use of evidence in policy and the focus on 'what works'. The chapter outlined significant political science contributions to understanding the evidence-policy relationship before discussing the more practitioner-focused literature on the barriers to the use of evidence. It then outlined the main themes and findings of research on 'what works' in a number of policy areas other than wellbeing, which partly informed part of the research design for the empirical material presented in this book, which is also outlined in this chapter.

Chapter 3 discussed the idea of wellbeing. It distinguished between competing conceptions of wellbeing, identifying the importance of the eudaimonic and hedonic traditions, and the implications these have for current debates on how and to what extent wellbeing should be addressed through public policy. Flowing from the hedonic conception of wellbeing, the chapter identified subjective wellbeing as a controversial but influential feature of current policy interest in the UK. The chapter also provided an overview of the rising interest in wellbeing internationally before turning specifically to developments in the UK, which have shifted from a predominant concern with measuring wellbeing to growing interest in understanding 'what works' for wellbeing in policy.

Chapter 4 turned directly to the issue of 'what works' for wellbeing, presenting the findings of original research exploring with policy-makers and stakeholders the key issues in the use of scientific evidence in relation to wellbeing in public policy. In doing so, it compared the role of scientific evidence with other forms of knowledge. This approach highlighted a broader understanding of 'what works' beyond the rational-technical sense often employed to describe the work of What Works Centres and the use of evidence more generally.

Chapter 5 looked at scientific evidence in the policy stream, drawing on the insights of the MSA and original empirical material to highlight additional themes in the use of wellbeing evidence. The chapter outlined the MSA in general terms before turning to the role of evidence within the MSA, suggesting that while evidence (as indicators) has a defined role in the problem and politics streams, it is rather overlooked in the policy stream. The chapter discussed wellbeing evidence in the problem stream before turning to a detailed discussion of its role in the policy stream and, in particular, its relation to the criteria for survival. It suggested that scientific evidence offers a potentially important resource for policy entrepreneurs in meeting these criteria for survival and thus steering wellbeing through the 'policy primeval soup'.

The remainder of this chapter drills down into some of the key issues raised by the findings of the book as they relate to each of the main aims.

Evidence and the Prospects for Wellbeing in Public Policy

As discussed in Chapter 3, the financial crisis and the failings that led to it opened a window of opportunity for new ideas and the rise of wellbeing has been a feature of this. A period of political uncertainty and unpredictability has followed the crisis as mainstream political parties across the world have struggled to align with the concerns of citizens. The most visible international manifestation of this unpredictability was the election of Donald Trump as US President in November 2016, while an important illustration in the UK was the unexpected outcome of the Brexit referendum in June of the same year.[1] This period of uncertainty has continued since 2016, not least in the UK, with the resignation of David Cameron as Prime Minister following the Brexit referendum result and a general election in June 2017 in which Cameron's successor, Theresa May, lost her overall majority in

---

[1] On 23 June 2016, the UK voted to leave the European Union, by 51.9% for leave, and 48.1% for remain.

Parliament; not least because of a surprisingly effective campaign by the Labour Party, led by former political outsider Jeremy Corbyn.

In a context in which Brexit continues to dominate UK politics, the issue of wellbeing in government policy—along with many other issues—has failed to gain high-level traction. Yet, as we have seen in previous chapters, developments in this field have continued beneath the radar of political debate and public attention. It has been a period where the focus has been on the accumulation of evidence to prepare the ground for moving the policy forward when the political conditions are more propitious. In the light of the material presented, this section reflects on the role of evidence in shaping the prospects of wellbeing in UK policy, addressing a number of key issues raised.

The Political Appeal of Wellbeing

As was discussed in Chapter 3, wellbeing as an abstract idea has considerable appeal. Indeed, it is counterintuitive to argue *against* wellbeing and politicians across the spectrum are ready to use the term to their advantage. However, as also noted in Chapter 3, the abstract idea of wellbeing becomes more contentious as more specific definitions of it are proffered. What is clear is that in the contemporary UK politics, wellbeing is used by politicians to mean different things for different purposes, as the following illustrations indicate.

In campaigning for Vote Leave in the Brexit Referendum, UKIP leader Nigel Farage (2016) stated:

> We must leave the European Union so that not only can wages increase for British workers but so that living standards rather than declining can start going up. The wellbeing of those living and working in our country matters to me more than GDP figures.

In taking this 'beyond GDP' argument further, Farage relates wellbeing to the cohesion of communities in the face of immigration.

Prime Minister Theresa May's use of the term has tended to relate to psychological issues and, specifically, mental health. The announcement of a package of measures aimed at mental health in 2017 illustrated this point.

> This is a historic opportunity to right a wrong, and give people deserving of compassion and support the attention and treatment they deserve. And for

all of us to change the way we view mental illness so that striving to improve mental wellbeing is seen as just as natural, positive and good as striving to improve our physical wellbeing. (May 2017)

Labour leader Jeremy Corbyn (2018) relates the idea of wellbeing to the issues of poverty and inequality:

> Our austerity economic model – purposely designed to exacerbate division and inequality rather than heal – is now having tragic consequences… Labour will transform the Tory free market approach into one that genuinely works for the majority of people, and makes sure the riches we have in this country are used for the health and wellbeing for everyone…

This is generally consistent with the usage of his most recent predecessors Gordon Brown and Ed Miliband, who saw wellbeing as most effectively addressed in material terms and equated it with living standards, although Corbyn also explicitly referred to addressing health inequalities in this context.

Liberal Democrat leader Sir Vince Cable has used wellbeing in a number of contexts, for example in relation to education policy he spoke of 'a new independent inspection regime, which values the overall wellbeing of individual children and the culture of learning in the school' (Cable 2018a) and in relation to economic regulation, suggesting that governments should 'look to break up enterprises where size is detrimental to the economic wellbeing of the country' (Cable 2018b). It is not clear in this case that there is a consistent or overarching use of the term, although Cable's Deputy, Jo Swinson has been a prominent figure in UK developments, establishing of the All-Party Parliamentary Group on Wellbeing Economics (Chapter 3) as a backbench MP and actively supporting the multidimensional framework established by the ONS.

Green Party Co-Leader Caroline Lucas (2017), not surprisingly, connected wellbeing to environmental sustainability:

> We know that infinite economic growth simply isn't compatible with a planet of finite resources, and we also know that the treatment of environmental concerns as "externalities" in pursuit of never-ending GDP increases is incredibly damaging. So if we know that growth is environmentally damaging, and not a guarantee of increased wellbeing, how do we shift our focus towards a new measure of a good society?

Other comments by Lucas in the same contribution suggest something of the challenges faced in securing wider awareness of developments in wellbeing measurement and evidence. She suggested that 'We need a new set of indicators that better reflect genuine wellbeing….' and 'It feels like Britain is ready for a real conversation about what makes for a good life'. These comments indicate either a lack of awareness of the ONS data and the public consultations that informed the approach taken or a lack of faith in the ONS initiative. Under a new leadership team in 2018, the Green Party proposed a *Free Time Index* to measure wellbeing, which was presented as an alternative to GDP (BBC News 2018).

These quotes illustrate the wide range of policy issues that wellbeing evidence might be sought to address. However, while political leaders across the spectrum are happy to use the term wellbeing, in none of these cases is it taken as the main purpose of policy: a development that some believe is possible. For example, in relation to the Left, White (2015, 5) has argued that 'Politically, wellbeing gives voice to desires for an alternative, a new moral economy, a counterweight to the excesses of capitalism in a world where the promise of socialism no longer seems credible'. While Seaford (2019, 40) has argued that wellbeing could 'provide a large purpose for a left of centre government, similar to the purpose that animated the Labour party in 1945, and enabling it to counter the politics of consumption and the politics of fear'. At the same time, wellbeing as personal experience provides opportunities for the political Right, as an idea that is seen to fit well with 'the individualist ideologies of late capitalism and their faith in the pursuit of happiness through choice in consumption' (White 2015, 5). Indeed, at one point David Cameron suggested wellbeing might provide a large purpose for a centre-right government:

> If your goal in politics is to help make a better life for people - which mine is - and if you know, both in your gut and from a huge body of evidence that prosperity alone can't deliver a better life, then you've got to take practical steps to make sure government is properly focused on our quality of life as well as economic growth…. (Cameron 2010)

However, despite the ONS programme and related activities (Chapter 3), this potentially radical realignment of priorities did not follow under Cameron. As Seaford (2019, 40–41) suggests:

I can't help thinking that if Cameron had had the temperament of Margaret Thatcher, things could have been different. Cameron's version of flourishing would have put less emphasis on redistribution, and more emphasis on traditional social institutions, than the left version. Indeed, some suspected his rhetoric was designed to distract from inequality. But it would have been as opposed to market liberalism as paternalistic Tories always have been.

So, in an age when there is wide acknowledgement of the misalignment between political parties and public concerns, why has wellbeing not become more central to policy? The lack of relevant, high-quality evidence demonstrating 'what works' for wellbeing is part of the answer. However, as has been discussed at various points in this book, even where high-quality evidence is available, ideas that are new to the table must confront deeply held values, vested interests and institutional inertia. Stevens' (2011, 250) ethnographic study of evidence use within UK government found that there are 'many policy discussions and documents that make explicit use of evidence, but few use available evidence that challenge the contemporary distribution of power'. Faced with these challenges, the ways in which evidence is communicated are crucial to its prospects for influence.

The Communication of Evidence

If the first step for wellbeing advocates is primarily to convince civil servants, wider audiences must also be persuaded if significant policy change is to follow. On this challenge, the research highlighted the relationship between Kingdon's criteria of public receptivity and public acquiescence. Here, there is something of a Catch 22 situation in which politicians are reluctant to embrace new ideas unless they see they have popular support, but this support may require politicians to lead on raising awareness and generating support for such ideas. Thus, where evidence is important in persuading civil servants and politicians of 'what works' for wellbeing in a rational-technical sense, it also needs to play a political role in helping advocates to raise public awareness and support. As one of Cameron's closest allies on wellbeing and former Cabinet minister with responsibility for wellbeing Oliver Letwin (2016) put it:

> These are subjects that are discussed inside governments, they are also actually discussed inside cabinets, and they are discussed between ministers from different countries in my experience. The place they are not discussed is on

the hustings and in the media in political debate and that's the transformation we've got to achieve. (Letwin 2016)

At the paradigmatic level, neoliberalism was seen to become dominant in part because of the clarity and simplicity with which it was communicated. It offered 'a clear narrative explanation and diagnosis of many of the problems governments faced, with the added patina of close links to economic science' (Mulgan 2005, 223). Interviews for this book signalled very clearly that if wellbeing is to provide a challenge to neoliberal goals, evidence should provide the platform on which wellbeing narratives are built: it provides policy narratives with credibility and legitimacy. As one Interviewee (#11) put it 'we require that evidence in order to craft a message... we have values that underpin our work, but we require the evidence in order to have a message'. Moreover, this strategy is also helpful at the level of specific policies. As one Interviewee (#9) stated: '...if you want to convince others, actually, this way of working will produce better results for x population, then you need to have the stories of how people did it, but equally you need to have the evidence that backs up your claims'.

In the MSA, the role of communicating evidence is played by policy entrepreneurs, who can come from any number of locations (Chapter 5). Part of their role in trying to connect the politics, policy and problem streams is to construct stories that frame the problem and their preferred solution in persuasive ways: stories that combine evidence with an appeal to values and emotions. Interviewees were clear that for this to be done effectively requires openness to evidence of different types and for advocates not to be bound by the idea of a strict evidence hierarchy. As one interviewee put it: 'obviously statistics hold quite a large sway... but they need the stories behind it, so they need the qualitative work either to help them understand what the statistic is saying or for them to be able to translate that into a real-world environment for their decision-makers' (Interviewee #11). Echoing the argument of the epigraph opening this chapter, another interviewee spoke of the need for evidence that is 'good enough': 'Is there a type of evidence that might be good enough to inform some sorts of decisions, but not good enough for other sorts of decisions?' (Interviewee #1). Moreover, while policy entrepreneurs have to negotiate the tricky waters of evidence hierarchies, they also have to recognise the importance of policy hierarchies, which may demand different types and standards of evidence: proposals that demand a paradigm change are inevitably more difficult to construct than those seeking new policy instruments or adjustments to instruments within a stable paradigm (see Chapter 3).

As noted in Chapter 4, the challenge of communicating evidence is more difficult in policy areas relatively new to the policy arena where there are fewer 'trusted brands'. In relation to wellbeing, the WWCW is seen not only as a vehicle for collating and disseminating evidence but is intended to provide an authoritative voice in the way that NICE does in the health sector: a development that would assist the work of policy entrepreneurs. As one Interviewee (#9) stated:

> I want it [the WWCW] to build a solid reputation so that if you're reading something that's got that stamp on it, that actually you don't have to worry about its robustness, its validity - that somebody's done that for you. You know, I can pick up something and go, "right, this is a solid piece of finding" and I can run with that

Other interviewees spoke of the role of the WWCW not only in transmitting evidence through established routes but also in finding new ways to transmit evidence. So that, as one interviewee (#5) put it, '... it plays its part in making wellbeing something more desirable or more attainable or more understood or generally people are more aware about it, which would be great because our level, as a nation, of understanding of this is at stage one'.

Such arguments emphasise the point that, as Knaggård (2015, 49) has argued, when it comes to the legitimacy that knowledge offers decision-makers, it is often not the quality of evidence per se that is important but the credibility or status of the broker. Put more strongly, in some circumstances suggested that 'the transmission of ideas is more important than their "production"' (Radaelli 1995, 116). Communicating the idea of wellbeing is not made easier by ongoing disputes within epistemic communities over definition and measurement.

The Contested Nature of Wellbeing

As noted in earlier chapters, wellbeing is viewed as a highly complex, indeed 'wicked' problem in which a number of issues remain contested. While the measurement of wellbeing has progressed in the UK and elsewhere, how wellbeing is defined and measured remains a central challenge in bringing wellbeing more fully into policy: and particularly in providing a paradigm-changing alternative to GDP. McGregor (2018, 208) has argued that 'If this fragmentation were to continue, then this would be a profound step backwards for the progressive hopes for a wellbeing paradigm. The paradigm will undermine itself with a proliferation of competing and contradictory data, founded in differing claims about wellbeing'. Central to this contestation is the tension between a single 'attention-grabbing' indicator that might rival GDP and a more rounded multidimensional dashboard approach. There are frameworks, such as the Canadian Index of Welfare (CIW), that provide a headline indicator that facilitates comparison of change in the overall index to GDP, while also allowing analysis of trends within different domains (Hayden and Wilson 2018).[2] Yet this tension is not simply a technocratic issue but is underpinned by different values that shape different wellbeing frames, and approaches such as the CIW do not resolve disputes in different contexts over what measures should be included in a particular index and how these measures should be weighted in creating a single indicator.

There is no technocratic solution to such disputes. Rather, as described by interviewees above, the need is for indicators that are 'good enough' for particular purposes. Echoing Kingdon's distinction between the problem stream and policy stream, Boulanger (2007) has drawn attention to the 'dramatisation' role of indicators in bringing attention to an issue, suggesting that indicators can play both a discursive-interpretive role and a rational problem-solving role at different stages of the policy process. He provides the historical example of the US unemployment rate as an indicator that has played both roles (see also Chapter 5): it was framed as a social problem so that a sufficient consensus could be reached outside about its definition, explanation and solution; it was institutionalised in public policy; and it remained present in public arenas, especially the mass media. The indicator and how it was constructed was not perfect, but 'good enough'.

For some, such an outcome is far from impossible for wellbeing. Former Cabinet Minister Oliver Letwin (2016) has observed:

> I think it is possible that in the future we will achieve a position where democratic politicians can get traction by reference to a set of data which are –

---

[2] Although it should be noted that this index is not part of national statistics, it is produced by researchers at the University of Waterloo. Moreover, it does not include subjective wellbeing, which many see as a vital component of any wellbeing framework.

even if in some senses naïve – nevertheless respectable and internationally comparable.

Boulanger's (2007) observations in relation to sustainable development (SD) indicators a generation ago have clear relevance for the closely related field of wellbeing. He identifies the challenge as one of maintaining the 'right balance' between the 'dramatisation' potential of indicators and their 'faithfulness':

> Despite their reluctance to do so, scientists and experts should strive to translate their controversies into a reliable yet resonant aggregate index in order to keep SD present in the main public arenas while helping in framing it in a reliable and consistent way. The challenge is to keep the right balance between dramatisation and faithfulness. On the other hand, if the discursive-interpretive stage (or facet) of policy-making needs few but resonant indicators, its problem-solving stage (or facet) needs several and less 'dramatic' ones. The challenge here lies in keeping a link between the aggregate index and the more mundane operational indicators. This connection is necessary if one wants to maintain SD as a fundamental objective on the agenda of the public arenas and avoid the risk of purely strategic policies and indicator manipulation in this area.

This argument about indicators echoes the point made above about the role of evidence in relation to stories that capture wider audiences: other things being equal, they are likely to be more persuasive if they are built on scientific foundations.

Yet even in the absence of a breakthrough on the indicators issue, which is particularly important at the paradigmatic level of challenging GDP, wellbeing developments have continued in a number of contexts, including the UK. These developments offer further insights into the role of evidence in taking forward the idea of wellbeing in policy.

Recent Developments

At international level, in 2016 the European Union launched its European Social Progress Index which aims to measure social progress for each EU region as a 'complement' to traditional measures of economic progress. The initiative is aimed at informing the development strategies for EU regions, although it is explicitly not intended to determine funding allocations, which are based on traditional economic measures such as GDP levels (European Social Progress Index 2016). In 2017, a group of governments including Costa Rica, New Zealand, Scotland and Slovenia agreed to launch the Wellbeing Economy Alliance to 'shift economies away from a narrow focus on marketed goods and services (i.e. GDP) to one more broadly focused on "sustainable wellbeing"' (Club of Rome 2018). Member countries intend to share good practice in wellbeing policy and champion wellbeing as the overall goal of development. This alliance has the longer-term goal of providing an alternative to international groupings such as the G8 and G20. Also in 2017, the Global Happiness Council was launched. This is a network of independent experts and practitioners from academia, civil society, business and government, chaired by Jeffrey Sachs of Columbia University. The Council oversees the work of six thematic groups (education, workplace, personal happiness, public health, city design and management) who are each expected to produce policy recommendations in the *Global Happiness Policy Report*, to be published annually and presented at the World Government Summit (WGS) in support of the Global Dialogue for Happiness (Global Happiness Council 2018).

At national level, the most striking development has been in the United Arab Emirates, which in 2016 created Minister of State for Happiness (from 2017 Minster of State for Happiness and Wellbeing) and launched the National Programme for Happiness and Positivity. The programme covers three areas: inclusion of happiness in the policies, programmes and services of all government bodies and at work; promotion of positivity and happiness as a lifestyle in the community; development of benchmarks and tools to measure happiness (UAE Government 2018).

Within the UK, there have been developments in the devolved administrations. In Scotland, a wellbeing approach informs the National Performance Framework,[3] with the 2018 framework stating its purpose as 'To focus on creating a more successful country, with opportunities for all of Scotland to flourish through increased wellbeing, and sustainable and inclusive economic growth' (Scottish Government 2018). In Wales, the Well-being of Future Generations Act (Wales) 2015 aims to improve the social, economic, environmental and cultural wellbeing of Wales. And, in 2018, Northern Ireland produced a draft wellbeing framework in 2018, although progress on this stalled due to political instability.

---

[3] The National Performance Framework was created in 2007 and later became more closely associated with wellbeing (see Wallace 2019).

In each case, policy-makers have drawn eclectically on different philosophical traditions and combined objective and subjective measures, although objective measures are emphasised in each case. All three jurisdictions have taken a dashboard approach rather than a single indicator, and for the same reason: that 'they believe that this is the best way to enable the use of wellbeing data in policy development' (Wallace 2019, 128). While aspects of the three approaches and the measures they employ overlap, they are driven by different purposes. In Scotland, this is performance management, in Wales sustainable development and in Northern Ireland political 'visioning'. Moreover, while all three include measures of personal wellbeing within their frameworks, they are not the same one. Wallace (2019, 131) argues that:

> These differences show that the development of the frameworks is an art, not a science; those involved are seeking to balance political priorities, available data and stakeholder views. In no case did the civil servants involved run statistical regressions or modelling to identify the 'best fit' indicators either to a dominant indicator within the domain, or to personal wellbeing.

These developments underline a number of themes identified above, not least the need for pragmatism in the use of evidence to suit particular purposes and contexts.

The key difference between developments in the devolved administrations and those at UK government level is that wellbeing measurement is brought into a broader framework relating to the purpose of government and each has an emphasis on outcomes. As such, these are seen as significant political developments. However, while there have been 'real social impacts' in Scotland, the overall policy effects in the three jurisdictions have been limited. Wallace (2019, 146) concluded that 'While there is evidence of a shift towards a wellbeing approach, it is not overwhelming. The activities appear to remain on the margins of public services rather than being a "golden thread"'.

At UK government level, in 2018 the Treasury further revised its Green Book guidance to government departments, to strengthen the position of wellbeing in the evidence-based appraisal and evaluation of proposals to inform decision-making. Specifically, it stated that 'Economic appraisal is based on the principles of welfare economics – that is, how the government can improve social welfare or wellbeing, referred to in the Green Book as social value' (HM Treasury 2018, 5). This change was described by the

WWCW's Head of Evidence as a 'subtle, yet important shift' that took wellbeing closer to the 'heart of policymaking' (WWCW 2018).

This shift appears to underline the position of subjective wellbeing within UK policy thinking (Chapter 3):

> Subjective wellbeing evidence aims to capture the direct impact of a policy on wellbeing. The evidence can challenge decision makers to think carefully about the full range of an intervention's impacts... The evidence can also help challenge implicit values placed on impacts by providing a better idea of the relative value of non-market goods. (p. 42)

However, while subjective wellbeing has been identified to perform a role in the appraisal and evaluation of policies, there remains caution:

> It is recognised that the methodology continues to evolve and it may be particularly useful in certain policy areas, for example community cohesion, children and families. (p. 42)

Taken together, these recent developments in the UK and beyond, alongside those referred to earlier in the book, indicate sustained interest and arguably increasing momentum in relation to wellbeing as a goal of public policy. Yet with the possible of exception of the UAE, these developments have yet to have a broad impact on policy. Moreover, the case of the UAE offers limited insights into the UK case because of the very different political systems and cultures. Developments in the more similar devolved administrations are, however, of particular interest for the UK case. These cases highlight the importance of political will in moving forward even where the science evidence was not fully in place either in terms of measurement or policy effects: the evidence has been deemed 'good enough' to get to the point of establishing wellbeing frameworks that go beyond measurement to expressing an aspiration for government. However, these frameworks have not been transformative in policy terms and a key challenge here, as in the UK case, remains that of more effective communication:

> The first challenge is to understand the key role of the wellbeing framework as a communications tool to frame the work of the governments. They tell us something about who we are as a society and where we are going. The communication is both internal to public services and external to citizens. Within public services, many will need convincing of the effectiveness of the

approach and yet scant attention is paid to providing those within the system with clear stories of impact that they can understand and articulate to others. Similarly far more attention needs to be paid to communicating the content of the frameworks to the public and sparking a conversation about social progress. (Wallace 2019, 146)

We return to this theme in the closing section of the chapter. Before doing so, we turn to the other aims of the book.

INFORMING THE BARRIERS LITERATURE

Chapter 2 outlined the case for greater use of policy theory in understanding the barriers to evidence use. The barriers literature tends to focus on issues in either the supply or demand for evidence and in the relationship between the two and not draw on theories of the policy process that highlight other important dynamics. This impacts not only the quality of the analysis but also the effectiveness of solutions proposed.

The application of the MSA to the case of wellbeing places the use of scientific evidence into the context of the wider policy system, drawing attention to a policy process that is characterised by ambiguity and uncertainty. As such, it provides a necessary corrective to assumptions of rationality that underpin much of the literature on the barriers to the use of evidence (see also Cairney 2016, 218). The MSA identifies different dynamics in the three streams and the importance of coupling the streams for significant policy change to take place. Applying the MSA in this case highlights the different roles evidence can play in highlighting a problem, proposing policy solutions and contributing to political and public interest. In different streams, the nature of the evidence demanded may differ according to the different purposes of different actors, as the discussion of dramatisation and faithfulness above suggests. The MSA identifies windows of opportunity when the impact of evidence is likeliest, and policy entrepreneurs as the key actors in the mobilisation of evidence.

On problem definition, the MSA brings attention to a number of key issues—values, comparisons and categories—each of which highlights a potential tension in the use of evidence on evidence. The first relates to the tension between narrow and broad-based definitions of the idea policy entrepreneurs are trying to sell to audiences with different values; the second to the tension between simple and more accurate measures in the search for comparability; and the third to the tension between categorising an idea as new or placing it within an established category to facilitate smoother but less transformative change.

In relation to the policy stream, the MSA identifies a 'primeval soup' in which ideas often 'float around' for many years but at key moments are more actively 'pushed' by policy entrepreneurs. In this primeval soup, scientific evidence has had a long-term effect of softening up the policy community to the idea of wellbeing as a policy goal, while the creation of the WWCW is an attempt to provide policy entrepreneurs with further ammunition with which to accelerate the process of policy change. More specifically, the MSA criteria for survival in the policy stream—technical feasibility, value acceptability, political receptivity, tolerable costs, and public acquiescence—draw attention to the very different types of barriers that new ideas must address if they are not to fall by the wayside. The case of wellbeing shows that through understanding the different demands of these criteria leads to a more nuanced understanding of the role of evidence at this stage of the policy process.

The multi-level approach to the MSA outlined in Chapter 5 draws attention to policy-making processes in which some policy areas are nested at one level and others where policy competence is shared across levels. It highlights the role of evidence promoters (policy entrepreneurs) as 'venue shoppers' seeking to sell their idea of the problem and their proposed solution in different arenas and are thus 'seeking to promote both temporal and *spatial* alignment of the streams (an idea whose *time and place* has come)' (Bache and Reardon 2016, 148). As such, this draws attention to the potential of ideas to spread between and across levels of governance. In the UK, devolution has created a system of multi-level governance that has increased the potential for policy learning between the devolved administrations (above). It is evident from Wallace's (2019) study of the UK's devolved illustration that elements of this have taken place, with the Carnegie Trust playing an influential role in developments in Scotland and Northern Ireland (see also Doran and Hodgett 2018). Moreover, a multi-level analysis draws attention to how 'the opening of a policy window at one level of governance can increase the possibility of the opening of a window in the same policy area at another level of governance (*spatial* spillover)', which suggests potential for greater policy learning between the UK level and the devolved governments. Such insights provide a more fine-grained understanding of both the barriers to and the opportunities for the use of evidence in moving an idea through the policy stream.

INFORMING THE MULTIPLE STREAMS APPROACH

This book has applied some of the MSA core concepts to the use of evidence in the field of wellbeing. In doing so, this has highlighted the role of scientific evidence in the policy stream: an aspect of the MSA that has generally been overlooked. In the case of wellbeing, scientific evidence is seen to have an important role to play in moving wellbeing from the governmental agenda to the decision agenda. As noted in Chapter 5, while the MSA literature often identifies 'information' as a resource, it tends not to distinguish between scientific evidence and other forms of knowledge, which offer different types of resources. This distinction is important in the case of wellbeing—and no doubt others—because scientific evidence has an elevated status among forms of knowledge that offers a particular type of legitimacy.

However, as noted at various points in this book, evidence by itself rarely leads directly to policy change and the MSA posits a wide range of factors that lead to governments taking policy action. These include the dynamics of the three streams and the opening and closing of policy windows. In particular, it identifies policy entrepreneurs as key actors in framing problems and proposing solutions and ultimately coupling all three streams. However, while it suggests that policy entrepreneurs use evidence in the form of 'indicators' to frame problems, it pays little attention to how they might use scientific evidence in the policy stream. This book has highlighted how evidence—either as indicators or in a broader sense—can not only have a long-term impact in softening up decision-makers in the policy stream, but, more specifically, how evidence can help demonstrate how ideas might meet the policy stream criteria for survival. As such, it offers a potentially important resource for policy entrepreneurs seeking to advance their ideas within the policy stream and ultimately in coupling the three streams. Recent research by Ritter et al. (2018, 1545) came to a similar conclusion: 'providing entrepreneurs with evidence and research may strengthen the opportunity to creatively manipulate the three streams (rather than assuming that the data will "speak for themselves")'. Thus, in the same way that policy entrepreneurs operating in the problem stream can use indicators to frame problems, in the policy stream they can draw on scientific evidence more broadly defined to help construct and communicate their policy solutions.

The findings on wellbeing evidence also indicate how the policy stream criteria for survival, rather than being clearly distinct, are often closely related. The relationship between political receptivity and public acquiescence illustrates this point well, but there are other examples (Chapter 5). The findings also illustrate the importance of political activity in the policy stream and thus offer another insight for the MSA. While Kingdon's analysis places considerable importance on politicians as recipients of policy ideas, the case of wellbeing provides an illustration of the important role politicians can also play in the policy stream through promoting the generation of evidence. As Prime Minister, Cameron launched evidence-generating initiatives that contributed to the softening-up process, most notably the ONS MNW programme, and the subsequent creation of the WWCW to collate evidence that would promote the idea of wellbeing as a policy goal: activity that challenges the MSA notion of stream independence (Herweg et al. 2015).

Finally on the MSA, this research points towards the increasing relevance of a multi-level approach. It is clear from previous research on the measurement of wellbeing that there are strong evidence flows across national boundaries and between levels of governance facilitated by established networks of statisticians, academics and others (Bache and Reardon 2016). This infrastructure provides the basis on which exchanges on the evidence of 'what works' for wellbeing in policy have begun to take place. Moreover, interviewees acknowledged the growing interdependence of levels of governance. As one interviewee put it: '…understanding those drivers at those different organisational levels and how you impact from those levels and how you work together would be quite a beneficial way of looking at it… how we do actually influence wellbeing through those different tiers?' (Interviewee #2). It is evident that in the case of wellbeing, which relates to a wide range of policy fields, effective policy action will inevitably depend on effective coordination between actors at different levels. As McGregor (2018, 197–224) argued, it is 'necessary to understand the interactions of agency and structure, across inter-connecting levels of scale, that constitute the processes, whereby wellbeing is generated or denied'.

Conclusion

Wellbeing is an idea that is relatively new to the policy arena and one that remains unsettled. It is a complex idea that faces particular challenges in an era of uncertainty and unpredictably in which simple solutions appear increasingly attractive. There are disagreements within epistemic communities about how wellbeing should be defined and measured for public policy purposes and other challenges relating to securing wider support for the idea as a policy goal. Yet the idea is being taken seriously by actors within UK government, and the accumulation and dissemination of scientific evidence is seen as a crucial next step in taking the idea further into policy. In this context, this book has considered the role of evidence in taking wellbeing forward in policy.

Despite the challenges faced, the fact that wellbeing initiatives have progressed during the period of research for this book illustrates that it continues to have momentum and that the scientific evidence available has proved 'good enough' to help advance developments in some contexts. However, developments to date have not delivered the transformative change that many wellbeing advocates seek. The dominance of GDP as an indicator of progress has not been seriously threatened, and there is no suggestion that epistemic communities are close to a consensus on a persuasive alternative that is rooted in a clear theory of wellbeing. On this issue, there often remains a significant gap between what scientists and statisticians would prefer and what politicians and the general public might find attractive.

However, the route to transformative change may not require a change in headline indicators. It is possible that this development may follow rather than lead change. Mulgan's (2005, 223) discussion of the spread of Keynesianism is interesting in this respect. He notes how the practice of Keynesian economics in different forms 'was separately "discovered" in New Zealand, Scandinavia and Roosevelt's US before, not after, the theory had been first formalised by Keynes himself. It was then popularised (some said bastardised) to become the conventional wisdom of the post-war era'. It was in this context that GDP emerged and became dominant as the key indicator for this framework.

There are parallels with wellbeing. Various initiatives have emerged in quite different places, and this proliferation of initiatives may bring forward the possibility of further change through policy learning. Wellbeing advocates generally view the prospect of transformative change as a long-term process in which, over time, evidence can foster learning, belief change and policy change (Weiss 1979; Sabatier 1987). Indeed, for many, this 'bottom-up' approach is the likeliest strategy for success: a gradual accumulation of evidence and practice that in the longer term reduces resistance. As one prominent wellbeing advocate succinctly put it, 'familiarity breeds consent' (Durand 2016).

Yet, whatever strategy is adopted to take wellbeing forward in policy, the way in which it is framed and communicated is crucial. A key argument of this book is that scientific evidence can make a significant contribution in this respect. It gives ideas substance and also offers legitimacy. Thus, following Hunter's (2009, 596) comments on public health, it is important to recognise that while promoting the idea of wellbeing in policy is both an art and a science, it should not be an act of faith.

REFERENCES

Bache, I., & Reardon, L. (2016). *The Politics and Policy of Wellbeing: Understanding the Rise and Significance of a New Agenda*. Cheltenham: Edward Elgar.

BBC News. (2018, October 5). Free Time Should Be Measure of UK's Well-Being, Say Greens. *BBC News*. https://www.bbc.co.uk/news/uk-politics-45750920. Accessed 4 December 2018.

Boulanger, P. (2007). Political Uses of Social Indicators: Overview and Application to Sustainable Development Indicators. *International Journal of Sustainable Development, 10*(1–2), 14–32.

Cable, V. (2018a). *Vince Cable Attacks Jeremy Corbyn for Failing to Stand Up for the Poorest*. https://www.markpack.org.uk/154252/vince-cable-southport-conference-speech/. Accessed 5 November 2018.

Cable, V. (2018b). *Taming the Tech Titans*. https://www.libdems.org.uk/vince_cable_speech_break_up_the_big_tech_monopolies. Accessed 27 December 2018.

Cairney, P. (2016). *The Politics of Evidence-Based Policy Making*. Basingstoke: Palgrave Macmillan.

Cameron, D. (2010, November 25). *PM Speech on Well-Being*. Speech Given by the Prime Minister. London. http://www.number10.gov.uk/news/speeches-and-transcripts/2010/11/pm-speech-onwell-being-57569. Accessed 9 January 2011.

Club of Rome. (2018). *Toward a Sustainable Wellbeing Economy*. https://www.clubofrome.org/2018/05/08/toward-a-sustainable-wellbeing-economy/. Accessed 4 August 2018.

Corbyn, J. (2018). *Jeremy Corbyn: Tackling Poverty and Health Inequality Is Labour's Next Great Mission*. https://labourlist.org/2018/07/jeremy-corbyn-tackling-poverty-and-health-inequality-is-labours-next-great-mission/. Accessed 28 December 2018.

Doran, P., & Hodgett, S. (2018). Societal Wellbeing: Catalyst for Systems and Social Change in Northern Ireland. In I. Bache & K. Scott (Eds.), *The Politics of Wellbeing: Theory, Policy and Practice* (pp. 169–196). Cham: Palgrave Macmillan.

Durand, M. (2016, December 12–13). *Subjective Well-Being over the Life Course: Evidence and Policy Implications.* Comments to Conference at the London School of Economics and Political Science.

European Social Progress Index. (2016). *European Social Progress Index.* http://ec. europa.eu/regional_policy/en/information/maps/social_progress. Accessed 6 August 2018.

Farage, N. (2016). *Nigel Farage: Why We Must Vote Leave in the EU Referendum.* https://www.express.co.uk/comment/expresscomment/681776/ nigel-farage-eu-referendum-brexit-vote-leave-independence-ukip. Accessed 3 November 2018.

Global Happiness Council. (2018). *Global Happiness and Wellbeing Policy Report.* http://www.happinesscouncil.org/. Accessed 8 August 2018.

Hayden, A., & Wilson, J. (2018). Challenging the Dominant Economic Narrative Through Alternative Wellbeing Indicators: The Canadian Experience. In I. Bache & K. Scott (Eds.), *The Politics of Wellbeing: Theory, Policy and Practice* (pp. 143–168). Cham: Palgrave Macmillan.

Herweg, N., Hub, C., & Zohlnhöfer, R. (2015). Straightening the Three Streams: Theorising Extensions of the Multiple Streams Framework. *European Journal of Political Research, 54,* 435–449.

HM Treasury. (2018). *The Green Book: Central Government Guidance on Appraisal and Evaluation.* https://assets.publishing.service.gov.uk/government/ uploads/system/uploads/attachment_data/file/685903/The_Green_Book. pdf. Accessed 10 November 2018.

Hunter, D. (2009). Relationship Between Evidence and Policy: A Case of Evidence-based Policy or Policy-based Evidence? *Public Health, 123,* 583–586.

Knaggård, Å. (2015). The Multiple Streams Framework and the Problem Broker. *European Journal of Political Research, 54,* 450–465.

Letwin, O. (2016, December 12–13). *Subjective Well-Being over the Life Course: Evidence and Policy Implications.* Comments to Conference at London School of Economics and Political Science.

Lucas, C. (2017, December 1). Why We Can No Longer Worship at GDP's Alter. *The Guardian.* https://www.theguardian.com/business/2017/dec/01/why-we-can-no-longer-worship-at-gdp-altar. Accessed 10 November 2018.

May, T. (2017). *Prime Minister Unveils Plans to Transform Mental Health Support.* https://www.gov.uk/government/news/prime-minister-unveils-plans-to-transform-mental-health-support. Accessed 4 November 2018.

McGregor, J. A. (2018). Reconciling Universal Frameworks and Local Realities in Understanding and Measuring Wellbeing. In I. Bache & K. Scott (Eds.), *The Politics of Wellbeing: Theory, Policy and Practice* (pp. 197–224). Cham: Palgrave Macmillan.

Mulgan, G. (2005). Government, Knowledge and the Business of Policy Making: The Potential and Limits of Evidence-Based Policy. *Evidence and Policy, 1*(2), 215–226.

Radaelli, C. (1995). The Role of Knowledge in the Policy Process. *Journal of European Public Policy, 2*(2), 159–183.

Ritter, A., Hughes, C., Lancaster, K., & Hoppe, R. (2018). Using the Advocacy Coalition Framework and Multiple Streams Policy Theories to Examine the Role of Evidence, Research and Other Types of Knowledge in Drug Policy. *Addiction*. https://doi.org/10.1111/add.14197.

Sabatier, P. (1987). Knowledge, Policy-Oriented Learning and Policy Change: An Advocacy Coalition Approach. *Science Communication, 8*(4), 649–692.

Scottish Government. (2018). *Developing an Environment Strategy for Scotland* (Discussion Paper). https://www.gov.scot/publications/developing-environment-strategy-scotland-discussion-paper/pages/13/. Accessed 12 December 2018.

Seaford, C. (2019). *Why Capitalists Need Communists: The Politics of Flourishing*. Cham: Palgrave Macmillan.

Stevens, A. (2011). Telling Policy Stories: An Ethnographic Study of the Use of Evidence in Policy-Making in the UK. *Journal of Social Policy, 40*(2), 237–255.

UAE Government. (2018). *Happiness*. https://government.ae/en/about-the-uae/the-uae-government/government-of-future/happiness. Accessed 8 August 2018.

Wallace, J. (2019). *Wellbeing in Scotland: Reframing the Role of Government in Scotland, Wales and Northern Ireland*. London: Palgrave Macmillan.

Weiss, C. (1979, September–October). The Many Meanings of Research Utilization. *Public Administration Review, 39*, 426–431.

White, S. (2015). Introduction: The Many Faces of Wellbeing. In S. White & C. Blackmore (Eds.), *Cultures of Wellbeing: Method, Place, Policy* (pp. 1–44). Basingstoke: Palgrave Macmillan.

WWCW. (2018). *Wellbeing in Policy Analysis*, Version March 2018. https://www.whatworkswellbeing.org/wp-content/uploads/2018/03/Overview-incorporating-wellbeing-in-policy-analysis-vMarch2018.pdf. Accessed 6 August 2018.

Bibliography

Allin, P. (2016). The Well-Being of Nations. In *Wiley StatsRef: Statistics Reference Online*, 1–6. https://doi.org/10.1002/9781118445112.Stat07996.

Allin, P., & Hand, D. (2014). *The Wellbeing of Nations: Meaning, Motive and Measurement*. London: Wiley.

Allin, P., & Hand, D. (2017). New Statistics for Old—Measuring the Wellbeing of the UK. *Journal of the Royal Statistical Society, 180*(Part 1), 1–22.

Austin, A. (2016). On Well-Being and Public Policy: Are We Capable of Questioning the Hegemony of Happiness? *Social Indicator Research, 127*(1), 123–138.

Bache, I. (2013). Measuring Quality of Life for Public Policy: An Idea Whose Time Has Come? Agenda-Setting Dynamics in the European Union. *Journal of European Public Policy, 20*(1), 21–38.

Bache, I. (2018). How Does Evidence Matter? Understanding 'What Works' for Wellbeing. *Social Indicators Research*. https://doi.org/10.1007/s11205-018-1941-0.

Bache, I., & Reardon, L. (2013). An Idea Whose Time Has Come? Explaining the Rise of Well-Being in British Politics. *Political Studies, 61*, 898–914.

Bache, I., & Reardon, L. (2016). *The Politics and Policy of Wellbeing: Understanding the Rise and Significance of a New Agenda*. Cheltenham: Edward Elgar.

Bache, I., Reardon, L., & Anand, P. (2016). Wellbeing as a Wicked Problem: Negotiating the Arguments for the Role of Government. *Journal of Happiness Studies, 17*(3), 893–912.

Bache, I., & Scott, K. (2018). Wellbeing in Politics and Policy. In I. Bache & K. Scott (Eds.), *The Politics of Wellbeing: Theory, Policy and Practice* (pp. 1–24). Cham: Palgrave Macmillan.

Bache, I., Bartle, I., Flinders, M., & Marsden, G. (2015). *Multi-level Governance and Climate Change: Insights from Transport Policy*. Lanham, MD and London: Rowman & Littlefield.

Bachrach, P., & Baratz, M. (1963). Decisions and Non-decisions: An Analytical Framework. *American Political Science Review, 57*(3), 632–642.

Bagshaw, S., & Bellomo, R. (2008). The Need to Reform Our Assessment of Evidence from Clinical Trials: A Commentary. *Philosophy, Ethics, and Humanities in Medicine, 3*, 23. https://doi.org/10.1186/1747-5341-3-23.

Bannister, J., & O'Sullivan, A. (2013). Knowledge Mobilisation and the Civic Academy: The Nature of Evidence, the Roles of Narrative and the Potential of Contribution Analysis. *Contemporary Social Science, 8*(3), 249–262.

BBC News. (2018, October 5). Free Time Should Be Measure of UK's Well-Being, Say Greens. *BBC News*. https://www.bbc.co.uk/news/uk-politics-45750920. Accessed 4 December 2018.

Bentham, J. (1996). *An Introduction to the Principles of Morals and Legislation* (J. H. Burns & H. L. A. Hart, Eds.). Oxford: Clarendon.

Blunkett, D. (2000, February 2). *Influence or Irrelevance: Can Social Science Improve Government*. Speech to the Economic and Social Research Council.

Boarini, R., Johansson, A., & d'Ercole, M. (2006). *Alternative Measures of Well-Being* (OECD Social, Employment and Migration Working Papers No. 33). OECD Publishing. https://doi.org/10.1787/713222332167.

Boarini, R., Kolev, A., & McGregor, J. A. (2014). *Measuring Wellbeing and Progress in Countries at Different Stages of Development: Towards a More Universal Conceptual Framework* (OECD Working Paper No. 325). OECD Publishing. https://doi.org/10.1787/5jxss4hv2d8n-en.

Boswell, C. (2008). The Political Functions of Expert Knowledge: Knowledge and Legitimation in European Union Immigration Policy. *Journal of European Public Policy, 15*(4), 471–488.

Boswell, C. (2012). *The Political Uses of Expert Knowledge: Immigration Policy and Social Research*. Cambridge: Cambridge University Press.

Botterill, L., & Hindmoor, A. (2012). Turtles All the Way Down: Bounded Rationality in an Evidence-Based Age. *Policy Studies, 33*(5), 367–379.

Boulanger, P. (2007). Political Uses of Social Indicators: Overview and Application to Sustainable Development Indicators. *International Journal of Sustainable Development, 10*(1–2), 14–32.

Bullock, H., Mountford, J., & Stanley, R. (2001). *Better Policy Making*. London: Centre for Management and Policy Studies.

Cabinet Office. (2015). *Government Guidance—What Works Network*. https://www.gov.uk/guidance/what-works-network. Accessed 8 September 2015.

Cable, V. (2018a). *Vince Cable Attacks Jeremy Corbyn for Failing to Stand Up for the Poorest.* https://www.markpack.org.uk/154252/vince-cable-southport-conference-speech/. Accessed 5 November 2018.

Cable, V. (2018b). *Taming the Tech Titans.* https://www.libdems.org.uk/vince_cable_speech_break_up_the_big_tech_monopolies. Accessed 27 December 2018.

Cairney, P. (2016). *The Politics of Evidence-Based Policy Making.* Basingstoke: Palgrave Macmillan.

Cairney, P., & Jones, M. (2016). Kingdon's Multiple Streams Approach: What Is the Empirical Impact of This Universal Theory? *The Policy Studies Journal, 44*(1), 37–58.

Cameron, D. (2010, November 25). *PM Speech on Well-Being.* Speech Given by the Prime Minister. London. http://www.number10.gov.uk/news/speeches-and-transcripts/2010/11/pm-speech-onwell-being-57569. Accessed 9 January 2011.

Christopoulos, D. (2006). Relational Attributes of Political Entrepreneurs: A Network Perspective. *Journal of European Public Policy, 13*(5), 757–778.

Club of Rome. (2018). *Toward a Sustainable Wellbeing Economy.* https://www.clubofrome.org/2018/05/08/toward-a-sustainable-wellbeing-economy/. Accessed 4 August 2018.

Communities and Local Government. (2008). *Practical Use of the Well-Being Power.* London: Communities and Local Government.

Cook, F. (2011, August 30–September 2). *Evidence-Based Policy-Making in a Democracy: Exploring the Role of Policy Research in Conjunction with Politics and Public Opinion.* Paper Presented for Delivery at the 2001 Annual Meeting of the American Political Science Association, San Francisco.

Corbyn, J. (2018). *Jeremy Corbyn: Tackling Poverty and Health Inequality Is Labour's Next Great Mission.* https://labourlist.org/2018/07/jeremy-corbyn-tackling-poverty-and-health-inequality-is-labours-next-great-mission/. Accessed 28 December 2018.

Costanza, R., Kubiszewski, I., Giovannini, E., Lovins, H., McGlade, J., Pickett, K., et al. (2014, January 15). Development: Time to Leave GDP Behind. *Nature.* http://www.nature.com/news/development-time-to-leave-gdp-behind-1.14499. Accessed 17 December 2015.

Davies, E. (2016, December 12–13). *Subjective Well-Being over the Life Course: Evidence and Policy Implications.* Comments to Conference at London School of Economics and Political Science.

Davies, H., & Nutley, S. (2002). *Evidence-Based Policy and Practice: Moving from Rhetoric to Reality* (Discussion Paper No. 2). University of St. Andrews Research Unit for Research Utilisation.

Diener, E., & Lucas, R. (1999). Personality and Subjective Well-Being. In D. Kahneman, E. Diener, & N. Schwarz (Eds.), *Well-Being: The Foundations of Hedonic Psychology*. New York: Russell Sage.

Diener, E., Lucas, R., Schimmack, U., & Helliwell, J. (2009). *Well-Being for Public Policy*. Oxford: Oxford University Press.

Dolan, P., & Fujiwara, D. (2012). *Valuing Adult Learning: Comparing Wellbeing Valuation to Contingent Valuation* (BIS Research Paper No. 85). London: Business Innovation and Skills.

Doran, P., & Hodgett, S. (2018). Societal Wellbeing: Catalyst for Systems and Social Change in Northern Ireland. In I. Bache & K. Scott (Eds.), *The Politics of Wellbeing: Theory, Policy and Practice* (pp. 169–196). Cham: Palgrave Macmillan.

Duncan, S. (2005). Towards Evidence-Inspired Policymaking. *Social Sciences, 61*, 10–11.

Dunlop, C. (2014). The Possible Experts: How Epistemic Communities Negotiate Barriers to Knowledge Use in Ecosystems Services Policy. *Environment and Planning C: Government and Policy, 32*, 208–228.

Durand, M. (2016, December 12–13). *Subjective Well-Being over the Life Course: Evidence and Policy Implications*. Comments to Conference at the London School of Economics and Political Science.

Easterlin, R. (1973). Does Money Buy Happiness? *The Public Interest, 30*(Winter), 3–10.

Easterlin, R. (1974). Does Economic Growth Improve the Human Lot? Some Empirical Evidence. In P. A. David & M. W. Reder (Eds.), *Nations and Households in Economic Growth: Essays in Honor of Moses Abramovitz* (pp. 89–125). New York: Academic Press.

Embrett, M., & Randall, G. (2014). Social Determinants of Health and Health Equity Policy Research: Exploring the Use, Misuse, and Nonuse of Policy Analysis Theory. *Social Science and Medicine, 108*, 147–155.

ESRC. (2014). *What Works Centre for Wellbeing 2014/15: Common Specification*. Swindon: Economic and Social Research Council. www.esrc.ac.uk/_.../what-works-wellbeing-common-specification_tcm8. Accessed 4 September 2015.

ESRC. (2017). *What Works Centres*. http://www.esrc.ac.uk/collaboration/collaboration-oportunities/what-works-centres/. Accessed 1 September 2017.

European Social Progress Index. (2016). *European Social Progress Index*. http://ec.europa.eu/regional_policy/en/information/maps/social_progress. Accessed 6 August 2018.

Farage, N. (2016). *Nigel Farage: Why We Must Vote Leave in the EU Referendum*. https://www.express.co.uk/comment/expresscomment/681776/nigel-farage-eu-referendum-brexit-vote-leave-independence-ukip. Accessed 3 November 2018.

Fujiwara, D., & Campbell, R. (2011). *Valuation Techniques for Social Cost-Benefit Analysis: Stated Preference, Revealed Preference and Subjective Well-Being Approaches: A Discussion of the Current Issues.* London: HM Treasury, DWP.

Global Happiness Council. (2018). *Global Happiness and Wellbeing Policy Report.* http://www.happinesscouncil.org/. Accessed 8 August 2018.

Goodwin, J., Jasper, J. M., & Polletta, F. (2001). Why Emotions Matter. In J. Goodwin, J. M. Jasper, & F. Polletta (Eds.), *Passionate Politics: Emotions and Social Movements* (pp. 1–24). Chicago: University of Chicago Press.

Gough, D., & Boaz, A. (2015). Editorial: Models of Research Impact. *Evidence and Policy, 11*(4), 450–489.

Griggs, S., & Howarth, D. (2011). Discourse and Practice: Using the Power of Well Being. *Evidence and Policy, 7*(2), 213–226.

GSRU. (2007). *Analysis for Policy: Evidence-Based Policy in Practice.* London: Government, Social Research Unit, HM Treasury.

Hall, P. (1993). Policy Paradigms, Social Learning, and the State: The Case of Economic Policymaking in Britain. *Comparative Politics, 25*(3), 275–296.

Halperin, S., & Heath, O. (2012). *Political Research: Methods and Skills.* Oxford: Oxford University Press.

Halpern, D. (2016, December 12–13). *Subjective Well-Being over the Life Course: Evidence and Policy Implications.* Comments to Conference at the London School of Economics and Political Science.

Hayden, A., & Wilson, J. (2018). Challenging the Dominant Economic Narrative Through Alternative Wellbeing Indicators: The Canadian Experience. In I. Bache & K. Scott (Eds.), *The Politics of Wellbeing: Theory, Policy and Practice* (pp. 143–168). Cham: Palgrave Macmillan.

Head, B. (2010). Reconsidering Evidence-Based Policy: Key Issues and Challenges. *Policy and Society, 29,* 77–94.

Her Majesty's Treasury. (2010). *Budget 2010 (HC61).* London: Stationery Office.

Herweg, N., Hub, C., & Zohlnhöfer, R. (2015). Straightening the Three Streams: Theorising Extensions of the Multiple Streams Framework. *European Journal of Political Research, 54,* 435–449.

HM Government. (2013). *Well-Being Evidence Submitted by the Government to the Environmental Audit Committee Well-Being Inquiry.* http://data.parliament.uk/writtenevidence/committeeevidence.svc/evidencedocument/environmental-audit-committee/wellbeing/written/1069.pdf. Accessed 17 December 2015.

HM Treasury. (2018). *The Green Book: Central Government Guidance on Appraisal and Evaluation.* https://assets.publishing.service.gov.uk/government/uploads/system/uploads/attachment_data/file/685903/The_Green_Book.pdf. Accessed 10 November 2018.

Hooghe, L., & Marks, G. (2001). *Multi-level Governance and European Integration.* London: Rowman & Littlefield.

House of Commons Science and Technology Committee. (2006). *Scientific Advice, Risk and Evidence Based Policy Making, Seventh Report of Session 2005–06* (Vol. 1). London: The Stationery Office.

Howlett, M., McConnell, A., & Perl, A. (2016). Moving Policy Theory Forward: Connecting Multiple Stream and Advocacy Coalition Frameworks to Policy Cycle Models of Analysis. *Australian Journal of Public Administration, 76*(1), 65–79. https://doi.org/10.1111/1467-8500.12191.

Howlett, M., Ramesh, M., & Perl, A. (2009). *Studying Public Policy: Policy Cycles and Policy Subsystems* (3rd ed.). Oxford: Oxford University Press.

Hunter, D. (2009). Relationship Between Evidence and Policy: A Case of Evidence-based Policy or Policy-based Evidence? *Public Health, 123*, 583–586.

Jaegher, C. J., Renn, O., Rosa, E. A., & Webler, T. (2000). *Risk, Uncertainty and Rational Action*. London and Sterling: Earthscan.

Jackson, T. (2011). *Prosperity Without Growth*. Oxford: Earthscan.

Jenkins, W. (1978). *Policy Analysis: A Political and Organizational Perspective*. London: Martin Robertson.

Johnson, L. B. (1964, May 22). *The Great Society Speech*. Delivered at Ann Arbor, MI. http://www.emersonkent.com/speeches/the_great_society.htm. Accessed 17 December 2015.

Jones, M. D., Peterson, H. L., Pierce, J. J., Herweg, N., Bernal, A., Raney, H. L., et al. (2016). A River Runs Through It: A Multiple Streams Meta-Review. *The Policy Studies Journal, 44*(1), 13–36.

Kennedy, R. F. (1968). *Remarks at the University of Kansas, 18 March 1968*. John F. Kennedy Presidential Library and Museum. http://www.jfklibrary.org/Research/Research-Aids/Ready-Reference/RFK-Speeches/Remarks-of-Robert-F-Kennedy-at-the-University-of-Kansas-March-18-1968.aspx. Accessed 17 December 2015.

Keynes, J. M. (1937). *The Collected Writings of John Maynard Keynes* (Vol. 21). London: Macmillan.

Kingdon, J. (2011). *Agendas, Alternatives, and Public Policies* (4th ed.). London: HarperCollins.

Knaggård, Å. (2015). The Multiple Streams Framework and the Problem Broker. *European Journal of Political Research, 54*, 450–465.

Kroll, C. (2011). *Measuring Progress and Well-Being: Achievements and Challenges of a New Global Movement*. Berlin: International Policy Analysis.

Kuznets, S. (1934). GDP and Well-Being "Key Quotes". *Beyond GDP*. http://ec.europa.eu/environment/beyond_gdp/key_quotes_en.html. Accessed 17 December 2015.

Labour Party. (1997). *New Labour Because Britain Deserves Better, Labour Party Election Manifesto*. http://www.labour-party.org.uk/manifestos/1997/1997-labour-manifesto.shtml. Accessed 12 December 2018.

Layard, R. (2005a). *Happiness: Lessons from a New Science*. London: Allen Lane.

Layard, R. (2005b, January 20). *Mental Health: Britain's Biggest Social Problem?* Paper Presented at the No. 10 Strategy Unit Seminar on Mental Health, London, UK.

Letwin, O. (2016, December 12–13). *Subjective Well-Being over the Life Course: Evidence and Policy Implications.* Comments to Conference at London School of Economics and Political Science.

Lucas, C. (2017, December 1). Why We Can No Longer Worship at GDP's Alter. *The Guardian.* https://www.theguardian.com/business/2017/dec/01/why-we-can-no-longer-worship-at-gdp-altar. Accessed 10 November 2018.

Majone, G. (1989). *Evidence, Argument and Persuasion in the Policy Process.* New Haven: Yale University Press.

Marmot, M. (2004). Evidence Based Policy or Policy Based Evidence? *British Medical Journal, 328,* 906–907.

Marston, G., & Watts, R. (2003). Tampering with Evidence: A Critical Appraisal of Evidence-Based Policy-Making. *The Drawing Board: An Australian Review of Public Affairs, 3*(3), 143–163.

May, T. (2017). *Prime Minister Unveils Plans to Transform Mental Health Support.* https://www.gov.uk/government/news/prime-minister-unveils-plans-to-transform-mental-health-support. Accessed 4 November 2018.

McGregor, J. A. (2015). *Global Initiatives in Measuring Human Wellbeing: Convergence and Difference* (CWiPP Working Paper No. 2). Sheffield: Centre for Wellbeing in Public Policy, University of Sheffield.

McGregor, J. A. (2018). Reconciling Universal Frameworks and Local Realities in Understanding and Measuring Wellbeing. In I. Bache & K. Scott (Eds.), *The Politics of Wellbeing: Theory, Policy and Practice* (pp. 197–224). Cham: Palgrave Macmillan.

Mill, J. S. (2001 [1863]). *Utilitarianism.* Indianapolis: Hackett.

Mintrom, M., & Norman, P. (2009). Policy Entrepreneurship and Policy Change. *The Policy Studies Journal, 37*(4), 649–667.

Moss, G. (2013). Research, Policy and Knowledge Flows in Education: What Counts in Knowledge Mobilisation? *Contemporary Social Sciences, 3,* 237–248.

Mulgan, G. (2005). Government, Knowledge and the Business of Policy Making: The Potential and Limits of Evidence-Based Policy. *Evidence and Policy, 1*(2), 215–226.

Mulgan, R. (2007). Truth in Government and the Politicization of Public Service Advice. *Public Administration, 85*(3), 569–586.

Nussbaum, M. C. (1993). Non-relative Virtues: An Aristotelian Approach. In M. C. Nussbaum & A. Sen (Eds.), *The Quality of Life* (pp. 242–269). Oxford: Clarendon Press.

Nussbaum, M. C. (2000). *Women and Human Development: The Capabilities Approach.* Cambridge: Cambridge University Press.

Nutley, S., Powell, A., & Davies, H. (2013). *What Counts as Good Evidence?* Provocation Paper for the Alliance for Useful Evidence, Research Unit for Research Utilisation (RURRU), School of Management, University of St. Andrews.

O'Donnell, G., Deaton, A., Durand, D., Halpern, D., & Layard, R. (2014). Wellbeing and Policy. Report Commissioned by the Legatum Institute.

ONS. (2012). *First ONS Annual Experimental Subjective Well-Being Results.* London: Office for National Statistics.

ONS. (2018a). *Personal Well-Being: Frequently Asked Questions.* https://www.ons.gov.uk/peoplepopulationandcommunity/wellbeing/methodologies/personalwellbeingfrequentlyaskedquestions#what-measures-are-included-in-the-personal-well-being-domain-on-the-measuring-national-well-being-dashboard. Accessed 6 November 2018.

ONS. (2018b). *Personal Well-Being in the UK QMI.* https://www.ons.gov.uk/.../wellbeing/methodologies/personalwellbeingintheukqmi/pdf. Accessed 7 July 2018.

ONS. (2019). *Measures of National Well-Being Dashboard.* https://www.ons.gov.uk/peoplepopulationandcommunity/wellbeing/articles/measuresofnationalwellbeingdashboard/2018-09-26. Accessed 22 February 2019.

Organisation for Economic Co-operation and Development (OECD). (2007). *OECD 2nd World Forum—Istanbul 2007: Measuring and Fostering the Progress of Societies.* http://www.oecd.org/site/worldforum06/. Accessed 17 December 2015.

Padoan, P. C. (2011). *Statistics for Policymaking: Europe 2020.* Conference, Brussels, 10–11 March 2001.

Petticrew, M., & Roberts, H. (2003). Evidence, Hierarchies, and Typologies: Horses for Courses. *Journal of Epidemiology and Community Health, 57,* 527–529.

Phillips, D. (2006). *Quality of Life.* London: Routledge.

Radaelli, C. (1995). The Role of Knowledge in the Policy Process. *Journal of European Public Policy, 2*(2), 159–183.

Rawat, P., & Morris, J. C. (2016). Kingdon's "Streams" Model at Thirty: Still Relevant in the 21st Century? *Politics & Policy, 44*(4), 608–638.

Reardon, L. (2018). Networks and Problem Recognition: Advancing the Multiple Streams Approach. *Policy Sciences, 51*(4), 457–476.

Rhodes, R. (1997). *Understanding Governance: Policy Networks, Governance and Accountability.* Buckingham: Open University Press.

Ritter, A., Hughes, C., Lancaster, K., & Hoppe, R. (2018). Using the Advocacy Coalition Framework and Multiple Streams Policy Theories to Examine the Role of Evidence, Research and Other Types of Knowledge in Drug Policy. *Addiction.* https://doi.org/10.1111/add.14197.

Rutter, J. (2012). *Evidence and Evaluation in Policy Making: A Problem of Supply or Demand?* Institute for Government Report. http://www.instituteforgovernment.org.uk/sites/default/files/publications/evidence%20and%20evaluation%20in%20template_final_0.pdf. Accessed 19 February 2015.

Sabatier, P. (1987). Knowledge, Policy-Oriented Learning and Policy Change: An Advocacy Coalition Approach. *Science Communication, 8*(4), 649–692.

Sanderson, I. (2011). Evidence-Based Policy or Policy-Based Evidence? Reflections on Scottish Experience. *Evidence and Policy, 7*(1), 59–76.

Sarkozy, N. (2009). Quoted in Davies, L. (2009, September 14). Sarkozy Attacks Focus on Economic Growth. *The Guardian.* http://www.theguardian.com/business/2009/sep/14/sarkozy-attacks-gdp-focus. Accessed 17 December 2015.

Sarkozy, N. (2010). Foreword. In J. Stiglitz, A. Sen, & J. P. Fitoussi (Eds.), *Mismeasuring Our Lives: Why GDP Doesn't Add Up.* New York: New Press.

Scott, K. (2012). *Measuring Wellbeing: Towards Sustainability?* Abingdon: Earthscan.

Scottish Government. (2018). *Developing an Environment Strategy for Scotland* (Discussion Paper). https://www.gov.scot/publications/developing-environment-strategy-scotland-discussion-paper/pages/13/. Accessed 12 December 2018.

Seaford, C. (Ed.). (2011). *The Practical Politics of Wellbeing.* London: New Economics Foundation.

Seaford, C. (2018). Is Wellbeing a Useful Concept for Progressives? In I. Bache & K. Scott (Eds.), *The Politics of Wellbeing: Theory, Policy and Practice* (pp. 97–120). Cham: Palgrave Macmillan.

Seaford, C. (2019). *Why Capitalists Need Communists: The Politics of Flourishing.* Cham: Palgrave Macmillan.

Sen, A. (1985). *Commodities and Capabilities.* Amsterdam: North Holland.

Sen, A. (1993). Capability and Well-Being. In M. Nussbaum & A. Sen (Eds.), *The Quality of Life* (pp. 30–53). Oxford: Clarendon Press.

Shepherd, J. (2014). *How to Achieve More Effective Services: The Evidence Ecosystem—Crime Reduction/Health and Social Care/Education/Early Interventions/Ageing Better/Local economic Growth.* Cardiff University/ESRC What Works Network.

Solesbury, W. (2001). *Evidence-Based Policy. Whence It Came and Where Is It Going* (ESRC UK Centre for Evidence Based Policy and Practice, Working Paper No. 1), Queen Mary, University of London.

Stevens, A. (2011). Telling Policy Stories: An Ethnographic Study of the Use of Evidence in Policy-Making in the UK. *Journal of Social Policy, 40*(2), 237–255.

Tomlinson, M., & Kelly, G. (2013). Is Everybody Happy? The Politics and Measurement of National Wellbeing. *Policy & Politics, 41*(2), 139–157.

UAE Government. (2018). *Happiness*. https://government.ae/en/about-the-uae/the-uae-government/government-of-future/happiness. Accessed 8 August 2018.

UN. (2015). *Transforming Our World: The 2030 Agenda for Sustainable Development*. https://sustainabledevelopment.un.org/post2015/transformingourworld. Accessed 29 May 2018.

UNCED. (1987). *Our Common Future: Report of the World Commission on Environment and Development*. New York: United Nations.

UK Statistical Authority. (2014). *Assessment of Compliance with the Code of Practice for Official Statistics: Statistics on Personal Well-Being*. London: UK Statistics Authority.

Wallace, J. (2019). *Wellbeing in Scotland: Reframing the Role of Government in Scotland, Wales and Northern Ireland*. London: Palgrave Macmillan.

Weible, C. (2008). Expert-Based Information and Policy Subsystems: A Review and Synthesis. *The Policy Studies Journal, 36*(4), 615–635.

Weible, C., & Schlager, E. (2016). The Multiple Streams Approach at the Theoretical and Empirical Crossroads: An Introduction to a Special Issue. *Policy Studies Journal, 44*(1), 5–12.

Weiss, C. (1979, September–October). The Many Meanings of Research Utilization. *Public Administration Review, 39*, 426–431.

Weiss, C. (2001, July). *What Kind of Evidence in Evidence-Based Policy?* Third International Interdisciplinary Evidence-Based Policies and Indicator Systems Conference, CEM Centre, University of Durham.

White, S. (2015). Introduction: The Many Faces of Wellbeing. In S. White & C. Blackmore (Eds.), *Cultures of Wellbeing: Method, Place, Policy* (pp. 1–44). Basingstoke: Palgrave Macmillan.

White, S. (2017). Relational Wellbeing: Re-centring the Politics of Happiness, Policy and the Self. *Policy & Politics, 45*(2), 121–136.

Wilkinson, R., & Pickett, K. (2009). *The Spirit Level: Why Equality Is Better for Everyone*. London: Penguin.

WWCW. (2018). *Wellbeing in Policy Analysis* , Version March 2018. https://www.whatworkswellbeing.org/wp-content/uploads/2018/03/Overview-incorporating-wellbeing-in-policy-analysis-vMarch2018.pdf. Accessed 6 August 2018.

Zahariadis, N. (2008). Ambiguity and Choice in European Public Policy. *Journal of European Public Policy, 15*(4), 514–530.

Zahariadis, N. (2014). Ambiguity and Multiple Streams. In P. Sabatier & C. Weible (Eds.), *Theories of the Policy Process* (3rd ed., pp. 25–58). New York, NY: Westfield Press.

Zohlnhöfer, R., Herweg, N., & Rüb, F. (2015). Theoretically Refining the Multiple Streams Framework: An Introduction. *European Journal of Political Research, 54*(3), 412–418.

INDEX

© The Editor(s) (if applicable) and The Author(s), under exclusive   133
license to Springer Nature Switzerland AG 2020
I. Bache, *Evidence, Policy and Wellbeing*,
Wellbeing in Politics and Policy,
https://doi.org/10.1007/978-3-030-21376-3

CPI Antony Rowe
Eastbourne, UK
August 20, 2020